RJ GRUNEWALD

READING
ROMANS
WITH
LUTHER

CONCORDIA PUBLISHING HOUSE · SAINT LOUIS

ENDORSEMENTS

"The Gospel is," as Martin Luther said, "the very heart of the Bible. And the Book of Romans is the very heart of the Gospel." And though we love Romans itself and would like to read and understand what Luther had to say about it, many of us find it difficult to press through the antiquated language and unfamiliar phrasing that was common parlance five hundred years ago. And that's where this wonderful book comes in. Helping the modern reader understand Luther's thought as he processed Paul's, this book makes deep theology simple and hopefully will open the door for new generations of believers to enjoy and cherish the truths that spawned the Reformation, particularly the shocking grace of God bestowed on shockingly sinful creatures.

ELYSE M. FITZPATRICK, AUTHOR OF *BECAUSE HE LOVES ME*

Martin Luther didn't just read Romans. He was changed by it. Romans left Luther undone by God's message of a totally free righteousness. It's the same message that lit a fire in Luther leading to the Reformation. What I love about this book is that it helps any and all join Luther in discovering and celebrating the message of God's extravagant mercy as it's uniquely presented in Paul's Letter to the Romans. Luther's world-changing insights are all there and easy to grasp, made even more accessible by RJ's personal and pastoral observations. Don't just read Romans, read it with Luther and let its message of a totally free righteousness change you too.

MATT POPOVITS, PASTOR OF OUR SAVIOUR NEW YORK

The Epistle to the Romans contains some of the Bible's richest explorations of the Gospel. Luther's commentary on Romans shows how great a theologian—that is, an expositor of Scripture—he is. In this book, RJ Grunewald serves up extracts from both St. Paul and Luther and then explains and applies them in an utterly fresh, contemporary, and illuminating way. With its three voices—those of St. Paul, Luther, and Rev. Grunewald—this book is a highly original, extremely readable treatment of our justification by Christ. Laypeople will read it with pleasure and give it to their non-Christian friends.

GENE E. VEITH JR., AUTHOR OF *THE SPIRITUALITY OF THE CROSS*

RJ has done it again. He has taken the deep and sometimes hard-to-navigate writings of Martin Luther and has not only given us a road map to understanding but also taken our hand and gently led us along the path. This book is rich. This book is relatable. This book is beautiful. Buy it. You won't regret it.

JESSICA THOMPSON, SPEAKER AND AUTHOR OF *GIVE THEM GRACE*

Rightly understanding the Book of Romans is critical to rightly understanding the entire Bible. RJ Grunewald's *Reading Romans with Luther* is a fantastic resource that will help you better comprehend the Book of Romans and give you the biblical understanding necessary to understand the depth of our sinful condition, the magnitude of God's grace and mercy, how to properly appropriate Law and Gospel, and how to correctly understand how good works flow from faith into the lives of believers without slipping back into works-righteousness. This is a wonderful little book.

CHRIS ROSEBOROUGH, PASTOR AND CAPTAIN OF PIRATECHRISTIAN.COM

Concordia
Publishing House

Published by Concordia Publishing House
3558 S. Jefferson Ave., St. Louis, MO 63118-3968
1-800-325-3040 • www.cph.org

Manufactured in the United States of America

LIBRARY OF CONGRESS CATALOGING-IN-PUBLICATION DATA

Names: Grunewald, R. J., author.
Title: Reading Romans with Luther / R. J. Grunewald.
Description: St. Louis, MO : Concordia Publishing House, 2017. | Includes index.

Identifiers: LCCN 2016030600 (print) | LCCN 2016031739 (ebook) | ISBN
  9780758654847 | ISBN 9780758654854

Subjects: LCSH: Bible. Romans--Criticism, interpretation, etc. | Bible.
  Romans--Devotional literature. | Luther, Martin, 1483-1546.

Classification: LCC BS2665.52 .G78 2017 (print) | LCC BS2665.52 (ebook) | DDC
  227/.106--dc23

LC record available at https://lccn.loc.gov/2016030600

2 3 4 5 6 7 8 9 10   25 24 23 22 21 20 19 18 17

CONTENTS

INTRODUCTION

When I was a kid, I dreamed I could fly like Superman. He was faster than a speeding bullet, more powerful than a locomotive, and able to leap tall buildings in a single bound. The Man of Steel was untouchable. He soared above the commoners—out of reach for those without superhuman abilities.

Lois Lane, the Metropolis journalist, made Superman touchable. She reported his feats to people who only dreamed of getting a glimpse of him in person. She captured him with exclusive pictures and stories, bringing the out-of-reach superhuman down from the clouds.

Most of us experience theology the same way. We are the commoners who can't reach into the clouds of the great theologians. We see their words soar far above our heads. Their words are powerful but out of reach.

We need more Lois Lanes.

We need the journalists who make the untouchable touchable. We need translators who make the complicated simple.

I want to be your Lois Lane.

As a Lutheran pastor and a Christian who has grown up in a tradition that has benefited from great theologians such as Martin Luther and C. F. W. Walther,[1] I have developed an appreciation for venturing into the clouds and devouring the writings of such

---

1   C. F. W. Walther was the first president of The Lutheran Church—Missouri Synod.

theologians that often seem out of reach. Some may consider these theologians just "boring dead guys," but I want to show you how they are so much more than that. Their rich, difficult theology has shaped me as a pastor and the way I do ministry.

Good theology was never meant to be out of reach. In fact, part of what made the work of Luther revolutionary was the invention of the printing press, which allowed his work to be more accessible than ever before. But now that we are five hundred years removed from Luther's lifetime, most of us find his works to be intimidating. He's important but daunting. His words are influential but usually left on a shelf.

Someone once advised me: "Comprehend high and communicate low." This book is aimed at helping you do just that. It's meant to introduce you to the work of Luther. It's meant to explain his words in a way that removes some of the intimidation.

In the preface to Luther's commentary on Galatians, Luther suggested,

> I myself can hardly believe that I was so verbose as this book shows when I publicly expounded this letter of St. Paul to the Galatians. However, I can see that all the thoughts that I find in this treatise are mine, so I must confess that I uttered all of them, or perhaps more than all of them. The one article of faith that I have most at heart is the faith of Christ.[2]

If Luther's commentary on Galatians is verbose, his commentary on Romans is even more so. That's why I'm writing this book. Everybody should read Luther. His writings and teachings repeatedly call people to return to the message of "grace alone." His theological distinctions help us behold the beauty of the Gospel while coming face-to-face with the reality of our own sin. But his works can be incredibly intimidating. This book is meant to take some of that intimidation away and guide you into Luther's works.

When it comes to the primary message of the Church—justification by grace alone through faith alone—the Book of Romans stands above the rest. Romans repeatedly points readers to the centrality of the Gospel. It also includes several important ideas that influenced Luther's teaching on topics such as *simul justus et peccator*, Law and Gospel, justification, and righteousness by faith. (We will explore each of these further.)

---

2 Martin Luther, *Crossway Classic Commentaries: Galatians*, edited by Alister McGrath and J. I. Packer (Wheaton, IL: Crossway Books, 1998), xv.

In the preface to his commentary on Romans, Luther emphasized the importance of this biblical book by saying,

> This epistle is really the chief part of the New Testament, and is truly the purest Gospel. It is worthy not only that every Christian should know it word for word, by heart, but also that he should occupy himself with it every day, as the daily bread of the soul. We can never read it or ponder over it too much; for the more we deal with it, the more precious it becomes and the better it tastes.[3]

WHAT TO EXPECT

There are a few things to note before we proceed with what I hope will provide a more approachable introduction to Luther.

First, Luther's commentary on Romans is an incredible, yet complicated, commentary. Therefore, this book does not contain Luther's entire commentary on Romans, but only pertinent paragraphs that go along with the themes outlined in the table of contents. The fascinating thing about Luther's commentary on Romans is that he never actually intended it to be a book. Luther lectured on Romans from 1515 to 1516, and his notes were then compiled into a commentary.

Second, I've tried to organize this book in a way that fits how I'd want to read a book. A traditional commentary follows the Scripture verses in order, but this book is more devotional in scope. Therefore, rather than providing a linear exploration of Luther's commentary, I've divided and rearranged it according to thematic teachings in Romans. I've also included the Scripture passages that Luther references within the text and divided it with headings and chapters to allow you to find the topics and sections easily.

Third, the art that accompanies the text is intended to reflect the beauty of Luther's incredible theology and writing. As you read, I hope you will pause and reflect on the phrases that are called out with artwork.

Fourth, this book is primarily driven by Luther's words, not mine. I have provided commentary to show how Luther's writings apply to our lives today, but my words and Luther's words are clearly differentiated.

Finally, as you read this book, I'd love if this moved beyond reading and turned into conversations.

---

3   AE 35:365.

If you want to connect with me for conversation about this book or anything else, I'd love to talk!

Twitter: **@RJGRUNE**
Facebook: **RJGRUNEWALD**
Website: **WWW.RJGRUNE.COM**

So how would I describe this book?

It's Luther, but for everyday life. It takes a work that was written hundreds of years ago and puts it in a package that is accessible for the average person, showing that it remains relevant in our day.

I pray that this book will bring you deep into the riches of the Gospel. If your experience with theology has left you burdened and beaten down with the Law, I hope this book gives you rest, as Martin Luther's theology in Romans is the antidote to "do more, try harder" Christianity. And if your experience with theology has enabled you to appreciate the riches of the Gospel, I hope this book will use the work of Luther to further soak you in the truth that your faith is in Christ alone.

———————————————————————————

To download an excerpt, view videos, and sign up for updates, visit
CPH.ORG/READINGROMANS.

EXPOSED

On the television show *Portlandia*—a satirical comedy centered on hipster culture in Portland, Oregon—one episode highlights a conversation between the characters as Carrie and Alexandra look through Fred's endless photo album of the places he's traveled. Fred says, "Everyone on the Internet? They're not having as great a time as you think they are." Carrie then comments to herself: "I guess people are just cropping out all the sadness."

We've become experts at hiding.

We filter our lives and crop out the sadness so that everybody sees a version of us that has everything together. We don't tell people we have a problem, we aren't honest about our struggles, and we do whatever it takes to cover our muddy tracks.

A couple years ago, my family went on a vacation to Disney World, and as people often do, we posted pictures of the trip online. Not long after returning home from the trip, a friend commented, "Your pictures looked so great! But did your kids ever melt down?"

Of course they did, but we didn't share those moments online. This is what happens on social media. There are the experiences we share, and then there are the ones we keep hidden. We select the pictures of the happy moments, crop them, and add the perfect filter, but nobody wants to see the moment when my son had a meltdown because he didn't get to ride the monorail one more time.

This is the unwritten law of social media: show the best version of your life and hide the mess.

This doesn't happen only on social media though. We do it all the time, in every aspect of our lives. For instance, when I'm in a small group talking about difficulties, I'll share some struggles so that I appear vulnerable, but I don't share the real stuff. I find a way to crop out the really bad stuff. Or I'll make a confession to my wife or a friend because I know that I should. But the entire time I'm trying to be honest, I still try to avoid being *completely* honest. I can't name the sin. I minimize the significance of it. I justify why I do what I do. In other words, I try to crop out the reality of the sin, and I put a filter on it to make it look better.

This isn't a new problem; it's been going on since the beginning. In Genesis 3, not long after Adam and Eve have sinned, they do the same thing:

> And [Adam and Eve] heard the sound of the LORD God walking in the garden in the cool of the day, and the man and his wife hid themselves from the presence of the LORD God among the trees of the garden. But the LORD God called to the man and said to him, "Where are you?" And he said, "I heard the sound of You in the garden, and I was afraid, because I was naked, and I hid myself." (vv. 8–10)

Adam understands that he's screwed up. He can't let God see him like this. What would God think if Adam and Eve were exposed for who they really are? Hiding is the inevitable result of shame—when our sin is exposed, we do whatever we can to cover it up.

Luther's explanation of the following passage from Romans makes it clear that God exposes us when we are in hiding. Yet He does so not to end us, but to give us a new beginning.

> Paul, a servant of Christ Jesus, called to be an apostle, set apart for the gospel of God, which He promised beforehand through His prophets in the holy Scriptures, concerning His Son, who was descended from David according to the flesh and was declared to be the Son of God in power according to the Spirit of holiness by His resurrection from the dead, Jesus Christ our Lord, through whom we have received grace and apostleship to bring about the obedience of faith for the sake of His name among all the nations, including you who are called to belong to Jesus Christ,

To all those in Rome who are loved by God and called to be saints:

Grace to you and peace from God our Father and the Lord Jesus Christ. (Romans 1:1–7)

LUTHER EXPLAINS THIS IN HIS COMMENTARY:

MARTIN LUTHER

The chief purpose of this letter is to break down, to pluck up, and to destroy all wisdom and righteousness of the flesh. This includes all the works which in the eyes of people or even in our own eyes may be great works. No matter whether these works are done with a sincere heart and mind, this letter is to affirm and state and magnify sin, no matter how much someone insists that it does not exist, or that it was believed not to exist.

For when we consider [our righteousness and wisdom] base in our own eyes, it will be easy for us not to worry about the criticism and praise of others, as God tells us through Jeremiah (Jeremiah 1:10): "To pluck up and to break down, to destroy and to overthrow," namely, everything that is within us . . . "to build and to plant," namely, everything that is outside of us and is in Christ.

God does not want to redeem us through our own, but through external, righteousness and wisdom; not through [righteousness] that comes from us and grows in us, but through one that comes to us from the outside; not through one that originates here on earth, but through one that comes from heaven. Therefore, we must be taught a righteousness that comes completely from the outside and is foreign.

RIGHTEOUSNESS

the state of being just or rightful
(a relationship in good standing)

When we've been exposed for who we really are, the Gospel exposes to us the One outside of us, who gives Himself to us. As we sulk in hiding, we turn inward and are consumed with nothing but shame and guilt. But when we look outward, it is Christ, working outside of and unconditionally for us, who covers over everything that we want to keep hidden.

Our unrighteousness is covered by a righteousness we could never find for ourselves; it's foreign to us yet given freely to us. This

Therefore, we must be taught a righteousness that comes completely from the outside and is foreign.

— MARTIN LUTHER

righteousness, then, also calls us out of hiding.

What would happen if we stopped hiding? What would happen if we were seen for who we really are? What if we were honest about what we've been keeping a secret? What if—instead of creating a cropped version of our lives—we let people see the real, unfiltered us? What if people saw in us what God sees in us?

Listen to how Luther says it: "Christ wants our whole disposition to be so stripped down that we are . . . unafraid of being embarrassed for our faults and also do not delight in the glory and vain joys of our virtues."

> For all who have sinned without the law will also perish without the law, and all who have sinned under the law will be judged by the law. For it is not the hearers of the law who are righteous before God, but the doers of the law who will be justified. For when Gentiles, who do not have the law, by nature do what the law requires, they are a law to themselves, even though they do not have the law. They show that the work of the law is written on their hearts, while their conscience also bears witness, and their conflicting thoughts accuse or even excuse them on that day when, according to my gospel, God judges the secrets of men by Christ Jesus. (Romans 2:12–16)

MARTIN LUTHER

The Law in this passage . . . means the complete law of Moses, where both the Ten Commandments and also the love of God and of neighbor are enjoined. How is it possible that they will perish without this law and that they have sinned without it?

We must be careful not to connect *without the Law* with the verb *have sinned* or with *will perish*. But we should understand it in this way: Those who have sinned without the Law, that is, without the Law contributing to their sins, without the Law giving them opportunity to sin. Thus *they will perish without the Law*. It means that the Law does not bring witness and sentence against them because such a law has not been given to them. They have a different kind of law. For every law gives occasion for sinning except when grace, love, and will attend the Law.

The will always remains opposed and would prefer to do something else if it were allowed to, even though it may outwardly do what the Law commands.

God . . . will reveal our innermost thoughts, so that there is no possibility to flee further inside and to a more private hiding

God will reveal... our innermost thoughts, so that there is no possibility to flee further inside and to a more private hiding place.

—MARTIN LUTHER

place. The thoughts will of necessity be revealed and open before the eyes of everyone, as if God wanted to say: "See, it's not I who am judging you, but I merely agree with your own judgment about yourself and acknowledge this judgment. If you cannot judge differently concerning your very own self, neither can I. Therefore on the basis of the witness of your own thoughts and of your own conscience you are worthy of either heaven or hell."

To be sure, from our conscience we get only thoughts of accusation, because our works are nothing in the presence of God . . . although it is easy for us to excuse ourselves in our own eyes, because we are easily pleased with ourselves. But what does it profit except that we are thereby convinced that we knew the Law?

Grace meets you in the shadows and calls you out of hiding.

We don't need to be embarrassed of our faults and failures, because Jesus loves us despite all our faults and failures. We don't need to cover up all our sins, because Jesus died to cover over them. We do not need to pretend we've got it all together, because Jesus didn't come for people who've got it together. Jesus came for the people who are a mess—the broken, the ashamed, and the hurting.

MARTIN LUTHER

If the heart of a believer in Christ accuses him and reprimands him and witnesses against him that he has done evil, he will immediately turn away from evil and will take his refuge in Christ and say, "Christ has done enough for me. He is just. He is my defense. He has died for me. He has made His righteousness my righteousness, and my sin His sin. If He has made my sin to be His sin, then I do not have it, and I am free. If He has made His righteousness my righteousness, then I am righteous now with the same righteousness as He. My sin cannot devour Him, but it is engulfed in the unfathomable depths of His righteousness, for He himself is God, who is blessed forever."

The Defender is greater than the accuser, immeasurably greater. It is God who is my defender. It is my heart that accuses me. Is this the relation? Yes, yes, even so! "Who shall bring any charge against God's elect?" It is as if he were saying: "No one." Why? Because "It is God who justifies." "Who is to condemn?" No one. Why? Because "It is Christ Jesus (who is also God) who died, yes, who was raised from the dead, etc." Therefore, "If God is for us, who is against us?" (Romans 8:33, 34, 31).

Because of Jesus, we can stop the lies we tell ourselves and others. Lies about how "we are not really that sinful" or "I'm really a pretty good person." Because of Jesus, we are free to come out of hiding. No matter how much you've kept out of sight, Jesus gives you permission to bring it out into the light. The Gospel gives life when guilt and shame have taken away every ounce of life.

> For I am not ashamed of the gospel, for it is the power of God for salvation to everyone who believes, to the Jew first and also to the Greek. For in it the righteousness of God is revealed from faith for faith, as it is written, "The righteous shall live by faith." (Romans 1:16–17)

The contents, or object, of the Gospel, or—as others say—its subject, is Jesus Christ.

This is the Gospel, which deals not merely with the Son of God in general but with Him who has become incarnate and is of the seed of David. In effect he says: "He has emptied Himself and has become weak. He who was before all and created everything now has a beginning Himself and has been made." But the Gospel speaks not only of the humiliation of the Son of God, by which He emptied Himself, but also of His glory and the power which after His humiliation He received from God in His humanity.

The Gospel is not only what Matthew, Mark, Luke, and John have written. For [Romans 1:3–4] states expressly that the Gospel is the Word concerning the Son of God, who became flesh, suffered, and was glorified. Therefore, no matter who writes and teaches it, whether Matthew or Thomas, and no matter in what words or tongues, it is the same Gospel of God. It does not make any difference how many books and writers teach it, because it is all the same thing that all are teaching.

The Gospel is the power of the Spirit, or the riches, weapons, adornments, and every good thing of the Spirit, from whom it has all its power, and this from God.

The righteousness of God is the cause of salvation. And here again, by the righteousness of God we must not understand the righteousness by which He is righteous in Himself but the righteousness by which we are made righteous by God.

Blessed Augustine in chapter 9 of *On the Spirit and the Letter* says: "'The righteousness of God'; he did not say 'the righteousness of man' or 'the righteousness of one's own will,' but 'the righteousness of God,' not that righteousness by which God is righteous but that righteousness with which He covers man when He justifies the ungodly."

The righteousness of God is so named to distinguish it from the righteousness of man, which comes from works. According to God, righteousness precedes works, and thus works are the result of righteousness.

Romans repeatedly exposes us to the work of God for us. Christ for us. Righteousness for us. Peace given to us. Forgiveness purchased for us. Death for us. Life for us.

The Gospel is for us. God exposes us when we hide in our sin so that He might expose us to something greater—a Savior for us. Our Savior doesn't worry whether our reputation might damage His; He knows exactly what our reputation will do to His reputation. He justifies us, the ungodly, because it's His reputation that changes us—it's His work that makes us righteous.

CHAPTER 2

THE HUMAN CONDITION

Within the Church, Christians typically recognize October 31, 1517, as the date the Reformation officially began. That day, Martin Luther nailed his Ninety-Five Theses to the door of the Castle Church in Wittenberg in order to stir up debate and discussion in hopes that the Church would reevaluate some of its practices. This wasn't an abnormal practice; the church door was commonly used as a type of bulletin board. Likewise, Luther wasn't the only one offering critiques of the Church. But due to the power of the printing press, the nailing of those theses to the church door caused the Reformation to go viral.

Because we see 1517 as the beginning of the Reformation, we tend to forget that the ideas that came out of the Reformation were cultivating in Luther's mind long before the Ninety-Five Theses were posted for everyone to see. As a monk, Luther wrestled with the practices and beliefs of the Church; years before the Reformation began, God was reforming Luther's long-held beliefs.

Beginning in the summer of 1515 and continuing through the summer of 1516, Luther lectured on Romans, one of the most important books of the Bible when it comes to understanding justification—the centerpiece of the Reformation. In these lectures, we find Luther already wrestling with the depravity of human nature, a distinction between Law and Gospel, justification by grace alone, and the reality that Christians are simultaneously saints and sinners.

For while we were still weak, at the right time Christ died for the ungodly. For one will scarcely die for a righteous person—though perhaps for a good person one would dare even to die—but God shows His love for us in that while we were still sinners, Christ died for us. Since, therefore, we have now been justified by His blood, much more shall we be saved by Him from the wrath of God. For if while we were enemies we were reconciled to God by the death of His Son, much more, now that we are reconciled, shall we be saved by His life. (Romans 5:6–10)

With a clear awareness of his own sinfulness—plagued by guilt and shame—Luther understood the perversity of the human heart. He understood that his sinfulness was deeper than his own choices, that sin infected him.

MARTIN LUTHER

If God should not test us by tribulation, it would be impossible for any man to be saved.

The reason is that our nature has been so deeply curved in upon itself because of the viciousness of original sin that it not only turns the finest gifts of God in upon itself and enjoys them . . . indeed, it even uses God Himself to achieve these aims, but it also seems to be ignorant of this very fact, that in acting so iniquitously, so perversely, and in such a depraved way, it is even seeking God for its own sake.

Thus the prophet Jeremiah says in Jeremiah 17:9: "The heart is perverse above all things, and desperately corrupt; who can understand it?" that is, it is so curved in on itself that no man, no matter how holy . . . can understand it.

What, therefore, is original sin?

First, according to the subtle distinctions of the scholastic theologians, original sin is the privation or lack of original righteousness. And righteousness, according to these men, is only something subjective in the will, and therefore also the lack of it, its opposite.

Second, however, according to the apostle and the simplicity of meaning in Christ Jesus, it is not only a lack of a certain quality in the will, nor even only a lack of light in the mind or of power in the memory, but particularly it is a total lack of uprightness and of the power of all the faculties both of body and soul and of the whole inner and outer man. And on top of all this, it is a propensity toward evil. It is a nausea toward the good, a loathing of light and wisdom, and a delight in error and darkness, a flight from and an abomination of all good works, a pursuit of evil, as it is written in Psalm 14:3: "They are all gone astray, they are all alike corrupt."

To think that original sin is merely the lack of righteousness in the will is merely to give occasion for lukewarmness and a breakdown of the whole concept of penitence, indeed, to implant pride and presumptuousness, to eradicate the fear of God, to outlaw humility, to make the command of God invalid, and thus condemn it completely.

And as a result, one can easily become proud over against another man.

This is why many people, in order that they may have a reason for humility, busy themselves with exaggerating their past sins and those that they possibly could have committed, and they do the same thing regarding their present secret sins, so that they may appear humble because of their attention to them.

Therefore, if anyone looks down on another man as a sinner, sin still rules him doubly. For since he himself is a sinner, he compares himself as a righteous man to the other person and thus makes himself a liar and does not realize as a sinner that he is a sinner.

This language is classic Luther. Luther described the human condition as man being curved inward upon himself. A friend of mine described this concept when she wrote,

> Sin is the slippery slope of me, me, me. As the roiling sea we each contribute to and are then forced to swim in—us in our hoodies with our ear buds in, blocking out any and all input that does not delight or serve us, perpetually curving in on a world of our own creation.[4]

While it might be *en vogue* to describe millennials as the "me generation," it's more accurate to acknowledge that the "me

---

4 Heather Davis, "Man Turned in on Himself," *RJ Grunewald* (blog), www.rjgrune.com/blog/man-turned-in.

Therefore, if anyone looks down on another man as a sinner, sin still rules him doubly.

—MARTIN LUTHER

generation" began in the Garden of Eden. In each and every generation that followed Adam and Eve, sin caused the human heart to say, "Me, me, me."

But what, then, do we do knowing this? Do we settle for our heart's default position and simply accept as normal our own selfishness? Of course not! Paul emphasizes that when he says,

> What shall we say then? Are we to continue in sin that grace may abound? By no means! How can we who died to sin still live in it? Do you not know that all of us who have been baptized into Christ Jesus were baptized into His death? We were buried therefore with Him by baptism into death, in order that, just as Christ was raised from the dead by the glory of the Father, we too might walk in newness of life.
>
> For if we have been united with Him in a death like His, we shall certainly be united with Him in a resurrection like His. (Romans 6:1–5)

The meaning of the apostle's words is clear. For all these propositions: (1) to be dead to sin; (2) but to live unto God; (3) to serve with the mind the law of God and with the flesh the law of sin, mean nothing else than this, that we do not yield to our evil lusts and to sin, even though sin still remains in us. This is the same as saying: (4) Sin does not have dominion, does not rule; but (5) righteousness does rule.

We are in sin until the end of our life.

We read in Galatians 5:17, "The desires of the flesh are against the Spirit, and the desires of the Spirit are against the flesh; for these are opposed to each other, to prevent you from doing what you would."

Again, in James 4:1, "What causes wars, and what causes fightings among you? Is it not your passions that are at war in your members?" And in 1 Peter 2:11, "Abstain from the passions of the flesh that wage war against your soul." And in this way all the apostles and saints confess that sin and concupiscence remain in us, until the body returns to ashes and a new one is raised up without concupiscence and sin, as 2 Peter 3:13 puts it, "According to His promise we wait for new heavens and a new earth in which righteousness dwells," as if to say that sin dwells in this present world.

Concupiscence—your new impressive theological word of the day. Concupiscence is the desire and the lusting of the heart toward sin. When you come across this word in the writings of Luther, he is expressing that sin is not simply something we choose to do or not do; sin is our nature.

We aren't sinners because we sin. We sin because we are sinners.

Sin is the disease. It's the infection and corruption of the human heart. The heart, which should run to God, runs to created things. The heart corrupted by sin fears, loves, and trusts in anything but God. The human condition is having a heart corrupted by sin; our hearts have been turned inward on themselves since the fall. This corruption creates havoc in our lives.

The Gospel is the antidote to this condition. The One who never was plagued by "me, me, me" gave Himself selflessly so that we might be united with Him in spite of ourselves. It's His grace that sets us free from the curse of sin and that frees us to love and care for the people around us.

A WORSHIP PROBLEM

Sin, when we boil it down, is rooted in selfishness. Sin, in its essence, is the worship of self. It doesn't look to the heart and desires of God; rather, it seeks our own needs.

And while most of us wouldn't claim to worship ourselves, that is exactly what we do by our decisions. Whenever God makes clear what we should or shouldn't do and we decide to do something different, we have a worship problem. We are worshiping our own intelligence—believing that we know better than God what's best for ourselves. We are worshiping our own feelings—seeking satisfaction in our own experiences rather than in God Himself. We are worshiping our own stuff—trusting in something or someone to make us feel safe, valued, or worthwhile.

As Paul begins Romans, he exposes our self-worshiping hearts. He exposes the hearts that have been given over to worship the created rather than the Creator. He exposes the sin that has been given over to passions and lusts.

For although they knew God, they did not honor Him as God or give thanks to Him, but they became futile in their thinking, and their foolish hearts were darkened. Claiming to be wise, they became fools, and exchanged the glory of the immortal God for images resembling mortal man and birds and animals and creeping things.

Therefore God gave them up in the lusts of their hearts to impurity, to the dishonoring of their bodies among themselves, because they exchanged the truth about God for a lie and worshiped and served the creature rather than the Creator, who is blessed forever! Amen.

For this reason God gave them up to dishonorable passions. For their women exchanged natural relations for those that are contrary to nature; and the men likewise gave up natural relations with women and were consumed with passion for one another, men committing shameless acts with men and receiving in themselves the due penalty for their error.

And since they did not see fit to acknowledge God, God gave them up to a debased mind to do what ought not to be done. They were filled with all manner of unrighteousness, evil, covetousness, malice. They are full of envy, murder, strife, deceit, maliciousness. They are gossips, slanderers, haters of God, insolent, haughty, boastful, inventors of evil, disobedient to parents, foolish, faithless, heartless, ruthless. Though they know God's righteous decree that those who practice such things deserve to die, they not only do them but give approval to those who practice them. (Romans 1:21–32)

They worshiped Him not as God but in the likeness of an image, and so they worshiped not God but a figment of their own imagination.

How many people are there even today who worship God not as God but as something that they have imagined in their own hearts! Just look at all our strange, superstitious practices, products of utter vanity.

We can also simply say: "They did not honor Him as God," that is, they did not honor Him as it was fitting for them to render to Him honor and thanks.

Look at the order and the various levels of perdition.

The first level is **ingratitude**, or the omission of gratitude. . . . Self-satisfaction is responsible for this, for it takes pleasure in things received as though they were not received at all, and it leaves the Giver out of consideration.

The second level is **vanity**. One feasts on oneself and on all of creation and enjoys the things that bring profit. Thus one becomes of necessity vain "in his thoughts," that is, in his plans, endeavors, and ambitions. For whatever one seeks in and through these gifts is completely vain. One seeks only himself, that is, one's own glory, delight, and advantage.

The third level is **blindness**. . . . A person becomes necessarily blind in his whole heart and in all his thoughts, because he has turned completely away from God. Since he is then lodged in darkness, what else can he do except the things for which an erring man or a fool strives? For a blind man errs very easily, yes, he errs all the time.

And so the fourth level is the **error over against God**. This is the worst. It leads directly to idolatry. To have arrived at this point means to have arrived at the abyss. For when a person has lost God, nothing remains except that he be given over to every type of turpitude according to the will of the devil. The result is that deluge of evils and blood-letting of which the apostle goes on to speak in the following passages.

By the same steps people also today arrive at spiritual idolatry of a more refined type, which at present is widespread. Here they worship God not as He is but as they imagine and think Him to be.

From this text we may therefore deduce that if someone surrenders to these passions, it is a sure sign that he has left the worship of God and has worshiped an idol, or he has turned the truth of God into a lie (cf. Romans 1:25). Those who do not "see fit to acknowledge God" (Romans 1:28) are branded in this way, that they are permitted to fall into all kinds of vices.

It is bad enough to change the glory of God into the likeness of an image. This is the sin of blindness, of lack of knowledge, or of an erring heart. But it is still worse if one does not only err in this way but in the perversion of one's heart also worships those images and adores a creature.

And as they have not glorified God, neither in their hearts nor in their actions, but have instead transferred His glory to something else and have thus become filled with shame in their hearts, so it is only fair that they should also bring shame upon their own bodies and likewise upon others on their bodies.

If you're anything like me, when you read these words from both Paul and Luther, you can watch yourself go up the elevator from ingratitude to vanity to blindness to idolatry.

I'll arrive on the first floor without much thought, especially when life is good. The moment things are going well, I like to take credit.

The promotion, my kids' good behavior, the compliments from my wife—they say something about me. My house—I work hard for it. My sermon—I nailed it. My family—I sacrifice everything for them. Notice what happens when you start your journey toward idolatry: you become the subject of all the verbs. You're the one doing the work. You're the one deserving the credit. You're the giver; everyone else is the recipient. A lack of gratitude is just an early indicator that you think you're God.

The second floor doesn't take long to reach once you've explored the first. When I have no need for gratitude, vanity is the natural overflow. Vanity looks for the glory and the fame and the renown. It's the desire that all things point to your own greatness.

The third floor is when you stop seeing. Blindness makes you ignorant to the call of Jesus. Blindness misses the fact that you are a called child of God and ignores the life that Jesus calls you to.

The fourth level is idolatry. It's when your fear, your love, and your trust cling to something other than Christ. It's when your identity is wrapped up in you, your accomplishments, and your stuff. It's when you cling to your own work instead of Christ's work on the cross.

There's not one of us who isn't familiar with these floors. We could be the elevator operators, sending people up the floors of all the sinful places we have been to.

MARTIN LUTHER

The apostle is interested to show that all were sinners and needed the grace of Christ. Even if the individuals did not commit all the vices, yet, because they individually were idolaters, they were (at least in the eyes of God) the accomplices and equals of all the others who had been given up in the worst condemnation.

Unrighteousness is the sin of unbelief, the lack of the righteousness that comes from faith. He who believes is righteous, he who does not believe is unrighteous. Thus a man who does not believe also does not obey, and he who does not obey is unrighteous. Disobedience is the essence of unrighteousness and the essence of sin.

Paul describes the true worship of Israel in comparison to the false, superstitious worship of Baal when he writes,

I ask, then, has God rejected His people? By no means! For I myself am an Israelite, a descendant of Abraham, a member of the tribe of Benjamin. God has not rejected His people whom He foreknew. Do you not know what the Scripture says of Elijah, how he appeals to God against Israel? "Lord, they

He who
believes
is righteous,
he who does
not
believe is
unrighteous.

-MARTIN LUTHER

have killed Your prophets, they have demolished Your altars, and I alone am left, and they seek my life." But what is God's reply to him? "I have kept for Myself seven thousand men who have not bowed the knee to Baal." So too at the present time there is a remnant, chosen by grace. But if it is by grace, it is no longer on the basis of works; otherwise grace would no longer be grace. (Romans 11:1–6)

[God's people] are called a "remnant" from the fact that they were left over, for God kept them for Himself. In this word we see a marvelous commendation for His grace and election. For God does not say: "They remained," although this is true, to be sure, but this act of remaining was not the act of those who remained but of God who kept them, that it might be a matter not "of man's will and exertion, but of God's mercy" (Romans 9:16).

Baal was an idol who was worshiped by rites with which I am unfamiliar, except for the fact that the Book of Kings tells us that he was worshiped by kissing of the hands, dancing around the altar, and cutting the skin with knives and lances. Yet the same passage expressly states that they did these things with a pious intent and under the pretext and with the zeal of the worship of the true God of Israel.

They worshiped the true God, but under a superstitious rite and name, and this was forbidden them in the command that they should not make for themselves any graven image or picture [cf. Exodus 20:4; Leviticus 28:1; Deuteronomy 5:8]. But misled by foolish zeal, they thought that a graven image was forbidden only if it was the image of a strange god, but if they attributed it to the true God and worshiped it under His name, then they were acting correctly. And as a result of this zeal they killed the prophets as ungodly for saying that any kind of image was forbidden, and all this with a pious intent and out of zeal for God.

Moreover, through the worship of Baal there was depicted a monstrous form of righteousness and superstitious piety which prevails widely to this day. By means of this, [many] arrogant individualists worship the true God according to their own ideas with most ridiculous zeal; with their excessive piety they are worse than the most ungodly, that is, for the sake of God they are the enemies of God, and for the sake of fearing God they come to despise Him, for the sake of piety they become impious, for the sake of peace, disturbers of peace, for the sake of love and holiness, jealous and profane, and for the sake of humility they become proud.

Each man occupies himself before men with grand works and acts of righteousness, and the more he hopes that these works will be well regarded by God and men, the greater is his fervor in doing them. For if he knew that they were going to be held in contempt, he would not do them; so great is his pride and his vain imagining. He cannot believe that these works might be regarded as "a polluted garment" (Isaiah 64:6), lest he be forced to feel and act on the same level with sinners, which is what he flees and hates with all his might.

Sin is a worship problem.

And while we might not participate in superstitious dances to worship Baal, we certainly have rituals, behaviors, and practices that reveal what or who we worship. Louie Giglio, pastor of Passion City Church and founder of the Passion Movement, described our idolatry when he wrote, "You simply follow the trail of your time, your affection, your energy, your money, and your loyalty. At the end of that trail you'll find a throne; and whatever, or whomever, is on that throne is what's of highest value to you. On that throne is what you worship."[5]

Sin is always idolatry.

Sin clings to something other than God and turns to it for worth, value, and acceptance. Sin seeks satisfaction in the creations of God rather than in God Himself.

Who do you worship?

5   Louie Giglio, *The Air I Breathe* (Colorado Springs: Multnomah Books, 2003), 10.

THE OLD MAN

One of the reasons I believe the Bible is because the Bible never hides the mess. The Bible isn't a book of heroes who've got it all together; the Bible is a book of failures who are heroic despite themselves. The Bible is filled with stories of people who aren't unapproachable. It's full of people just like me—sometimes people who even seem way worse than me.

Moses is corrupted by a heart that leads to murder.

David's depravity is displayed in his affair with a married woman and in the cover-up of a murder.

The nation of Israel repeatedly finds itself in a self-chosen cycle of sin, slavery, and tragedy.

On every page of Scripture, we find a common problem with humanity. The human nature is corrupted by sin. Sin has tainted the most legendary of Bible characters with jealousy, rebellion, and scandals. The problem with all of the sinners who litter the pages of Scripture is the same problem with every one of us: the old man.

And there's only one way to fix the old man. He needs to die so that he might be made new.

We know that our old self was crucified with Him in order that the body of sin might be brought to nothing, so that we would no longer be enslaved to sin. For one who has died has been set free from sin. Now if we have died with Christ, we believe that we will also live with Him. We know that Christ, being raised from the dead, will never die again; death no longer has dominion over Him. For the death He died He died to sin, once for all, but the life He lives He lives to God. So you also must consider yourselves dead to sin and alive to God in Christ Jesus. (Romans 6:6–11)

MARTIN LUTHER

The term "old man" describes what kind of person is born of Adam, not according to his nature but according to the defect of his nature. For his nature is good, but the defect is evil. However, the term "old man" is used not only because he performs the works of the flesh but more especially when he acts righteously and practices wisdom and exercises himself in all spiritual good works, even to the point of loving and worshiping God Himself. The reason for this is that in all these things he "enjoys" the gifts of God and "uses" God.[6]

Nor can he be freed of his perversity (which in the Scriptures is called curvedness, iniquity, and crookedness) except by the grace of God. Ecclesiastes 1:15: "The perverse are hard to be corrected." This is said not only because of the stubbornness of perverse people but particularly because of the extremely deep infection of this inherited weakness and original poison, by which a man seeks his own advantage even in God Himself because of his love of concupiscence.

This iniquity is so bottomless that no one can ever understand its depth, and in Scripture, by the grace of God, not the iniquity itself but only the love of it is rebuked. Psalm 11:5: "His soul hates him that loves iniquity." And Psalm 32:6: "Therefore," that is, because of iniquity, "let everyone who is godly offer prayer to Thee," because He hates iniquity.

The "me, me, me" that corrupts the human heart is the heart of the "old man." The old man lives for himself—never for others. The old man is corrupted in his heart, curved inward on himself. The old man worships himself and what he owns as God.

The Christian life is the battle between the old and the new. The old man is the man that is drowned in the waters of Baptism. The old man is the man who is crucified with Christ. The old man is the man

---

6   Luther is no doubt indebted to Augustine's discussion of the difference between "using" (*uti*) and "enjoying" (*frui*) in *De doctrina Christiana*, I, 3–5, 22 (*Patrologia, Series Latina*, XXXIV, 20, 26), where Augustine compares the Christian pilgrim to a traveler far from home who "uses" a conveyance to return home but does not "enjoy" the journey for its own sake. In the same way, says Augustine, "If we wish to return to our Father's home, this world must be used, not enjoyed. . . . The true objects of enjoyment are the Father and the Son and the Holy Spirit, who are at the same time the Trinity, one Being."

who is stubborn and self-righteous and who seeks salvation by his own efforts.

But it's the new man who is born in the waters of Baptism. It's the new man who is resurrected. It's the new man who has empty hands, clinging to nothing but the work of Jesus. It's what Paul describes in 2 Corinthians 5:17, when he writes, "If anyone is in Christ, he is a new creation. The old has passed away; behold, the new has come."

As Paul writes in Romans, and Luther lectures on Romans, we find this constant battle between the old and the new. The Law continues to hold man captive, and because of the old man, we stand condemned by the accusation of the Law. Yet at the same time, we are made new by Jesus. We are no longer condemned, because Jesus fulfills the Law on our behalf. The sinfulness of the old man doesn't rule us; the grace that makes us new rules over us— not with dominion and power, but with peace and comfort.

> Let not sin therefore reign in your mortal body, to make you obey its passions. Do not present your members to sin as instruments for unrighteousness, but present yourselves to God as those who have been brought from death to life, and your members to God as instruments for righteousness. For sin will have no dominion over you, since you are not under law but under grace. (Romans 6:12–14)

MARTIN LUTHER

Sin has dominion over all those who are under the Law.

We must note that the apostle's mode of speaking appears unusual and strange to those who do not understand it. For those people understand the expression "to be under the Law" as being the same as having a law according to which one must live. But the apostle understands the words "to be under the Law" as equivalent to not fulfilling the Law, as being guilty of disobeying the Law, as being a debtor and a transgressor, in that the Law has the power of accusing and damning a person and lording it over him, but it does not have the power to enable him to satisfy the Law or overcome it.

And thus as long as the Law rules, sin also has dominion and holds man captive.

> So then, brothers, we are debtors, not to the flesh, to live according to the flesh. For if you live according to the flesh you will die, but if by the Spirit you put to death the deeds of the body, you will live. For all who are led by the Spirit of God are sons of God. For you did not receive the spirit of slavery to fall

back into fear, but you have received the Spirit of adoption as sons, by whom we cry, "Abba! Father!" The Spirit Himself bears witness with our spirit that we are children of God, and if children, then heirs—heirs of God and fellow heirs with Christ, provided we suffer with Him in order that we may also be glorified with Him. (Romans 8:12–17)

MARTIN LUTHER

All men are slaves of sin, because all commit sin.

In two ways this spirit [of slavery] is called the spirit of "fear." First, because it compelled unwilling men to do the works of the Law because of fear and the threats of punishment, and thus . . . in their heart they drew back from the intent and purpose of the Law the more they were compelled to approach it outwardly and in works. Second, this spirit is called the spirit of fear because this slavish fear also compels men to give up their outward obedience to the works of the Law in the time of trial. This fear ought to be called a worldly fear rather than a slavish fear, for it is not a matter of fulfilling the Law but the slavish fear of losing temporal goods or of suffering impending evils, and thus even worse than slavish fear.

But in another and better way, this spirit is the action of the "prudence of the flesh" that dreads the Law; it arises when the Law is laid down and recognized but is quiet before the Law becomes known. This is symbolized in Exodus 4, where Moses fled in terror at the staff which, thrown down, was turned into a serpent. The same thing happens when the Law is proclaimed to a man who is ignorant of the Law and is accustomed to breaking it; he becomes sorrowful and is irked by the Law, grieving over the lost liberty which is now cut off for him.

This is the spirit of fear.

A "spirit of fear" is what you experience when you don't trust that God has your best interest in mind. When you go along with the rules because you're afraid you'll get caught, that's a spirit of fear. When you are obedient only when it's convenient, that's a spirit of fear. When you begrudgingly submit to the Law because it's the Law, even though you don't want to obey—that's a spirit of fear.

The spirit of fear comes when the old man believes he knows what's best. But this fear flees when the Father calls the old man "son." The slavish fears that control the old man disappear when God adopts him as His own; the new man rejoices in the freedom that comes when God is both a friend and a father.

And [the apostle Paul] says: *to fall back into fear*. It is as if he were saying: "Before this you were in the spirit of fear and under a taskmaster, that drove you on, namely, under the Law. Now that you have been freed, you have not received this spirit of fear a second time, but rather the spirit of sonship in trusting faith." And he describes this faith in most significant words, namely, *when we cry Abba! Father!*

Fear does not say *Abba*, but rather it hates and flees from the Father as from an enemy and mutters against Him as a tyrant. For those people who are in the spirit of fear and not in the spirit of adoption do not taste how sweet the Lord is, but rather He appears to them as harsh and hard, and in their heart they call Him a virtual tyrant.

Such are the people who are displeased that God accepts no man's merits but has free mercy. They ought to rejoice because He has not put our hope in ourselves but only in Himself, in His mercy.

All who are of this mind are secretly saying in their hearts, "God acts in a tyrannical manner, He is not a Father, but an enemy," which is also true. But they do not know that one must agree with this enemy and that thus, and only thus, He becomes a friend and a Father.

As parents of two young children, my wife and I have decided certain rules are simply necessary. Our candy-loving children would gleefully begin every morning with a healthy breakfast of jelly beans, chocolate squares, and peanut butter cups (especially following any holiday that offers an absurd amount of free candy). Therefore, in our house, we've enacted a rule in these situations: no candy for meals.

I know what you're probably thinking at this point. How could I be such a cruel father? What kind of tyrannical father decides to take away the freedom of his children by robbing their joy of candy in the morning? What better way could there be to start the day than candy for breakfast?

Of course, you would never *really* ask such questions, because you have no problem understanding that the rule in this situation is meant for the benefit of my children. It's not about tyranny; it's about love for my children. It's not about robbing them of their freedom; it's about promoting it.

For some reason, when it comes to our relationship with God, which is described as a parent-child relationship, we have difficulty understanding this same concept. God's rules aren't those of a tyrant trying to rob us of our freedom, they are the rules of a loving Father trying to do what's best for us.

God accepts no man's merits but has free mercy. They ought to rejoice because He has not put our hope in ourselves but only in Himself in His mercy.

-MARTIN LUTHER

For He will not come around to our way of thinking and be changed for us, so that we may become His friends and sons. Therefore we do not have to fear Him nor any of the things which He wills and loves.

But this cannot happen unless we have His spirit, so that in the same spirit we love the same things which He loves and hate the things which He hates in the same way that He does. For we cannot love those things which God loves unless we have the love and will and spirit which He has. For if there must be conformity in the things to be loved, there must also be conformity in the feeling of love. And those people are called godlike men and sons of God because they are led by the Spirit of God.

The difference between these two classes of people is symbolized on the one hand by those who gave Christ vinegar, or wine mixed with gall and myrrh at the time of His passion, and on the other hand by those from whom He received a piece of fish and a honeycomb after His resurrection.

For the first class signifies that God is more bitter than gall and myrrh. Therefore they give Him what they have, that is, a bitter, sour, and sad heart, that is, a heart without hope. And when the Lord tastes it, He will not drink.

Of the first group it says in Jeremiah 15:10: "All of them curse Me, says the Lord," and Isaiah 8:21: "They will curse their king and their God." Or is this not cursing—to think in our hearts that God is an enemy and an adversary, to oppose Him in feeling and will, and, if possible, to take a stand against Him with all of our powers?

But the people in the second class, because God is like honey and the honeycomb to them, they offer Him this sweet happiness of heart, which He takes and eats in the presence of them all.

Galatians 4:6: "And because you are sons, God has sent the Spirit of His Son into our hearts, crying, 'Abba! Father!' So through God you are no longer a slave, but a son, and if a son, then an heir."

The way God sees you is not merited by your efforts or your intentions. God sees you as a son or daughter solely on account of the work of Jesus. Grace is the pronouncement of your relationship to the Father, and it has nothing to do with whether you are a well-behaved child of the Father.

By the grace of God, slaves become sons and daughters. Those held captive in their disobedience have been set free by the obedience of Jesus.

Paul, then, in light of the Gospel, will raise the question, "Now what? What does the freedom of the Gospel look like when we try to live as sons and daughters?"

> What then? Are we to sin because we are not under law but under grace? By no means! Do you not know that if you present yourselves to anyone as obedient slaves, you are slaves of the one whom you obey, either of sin, which leads to death, or of obedience, which leads to righteousness? But thanks be to God, that you who were once slaves of sin have become obedient from the heart to the standard of teaching to which you were committed, and, having been set free from sin, have become slaves of righteousness. I am speaking in human terms, because of your natural limitations. For just as you once presented your members as slaves to impurity and to lawlessness leading to more lawlessness, so now present your members as slaves to righteousness leading to sanctification.
>
> For when you were slaves of sin, you were free in regard to righteousness. But what fruit were you getting at that time from the things of which you are now ashamed? For the end of those things is death. But now that you have been set free from sin and have become slaves of God, the fruit you get leads to sanctification and its end, eternal life. For the wages of sin is death, but the free gift of God is eternal life in Christ Jesus our Lord. (Romans 6:15–23)

First Corinthians 15:56 tells us: "The sting of death is sin, and the power of sin is the Law." Sin is so powerful and has such dominion because the Law has dominion. Sin is the sting or power of death, through which death is powerful and holds dominion. The Law is the power or strength of sin, through which sin remains and holds dominion. And from this dominion of the Law and sin no one can be liberated except through Christ.

He who fears death more than Christ and loves his life more than Christ does not yet possess Christ through true faith. For sin has dominion over him, and he is still under the Law.

We must fully understand this, as He Himself explains it when He says [in] John 12:25: "He who loves his life loses it," and in another place (Matthew 10:37): "He who loves father or mother more than Me is not worthy of Me," and again (Matthew 10:38): "He who does not take his cross and follow Me is not worthy of Me."

As long as sin only attacks but does not gain dominion over the saints, it is compelled to serve them. In all these instances the hatred of the spiritual man increases more and more against the thing which is attacking him. Thus temptation is a most useful thing. Temptation becomes a servant when we resist it, because it then produces a hatred of iniquity and a love of righteousness.

God has arranged to remove through Christ whatever the devil brought in through Adam. And it was the devil who brought in sin and death. Therefore God brought about the death of death and the sin of sin, the poison of poison, the captivity of captivity. As He says through Hosea (13:14): "O Death, I will be your death; O Hell, I will be your bite."

This is the principal theme in Scripture.

These are the works of the Lord in which He delights and causes us to delight, as it is written: "The Lord shall rejoice in His works" (Psalm 104:31). And later on, in Romans 8:3, he says: "For sin He condemned sin." The Spirit uses these negative expressions which are sweeter than the affirmative ones to describe the eternal nature of the things about which He is speaking. Because for death to be killed means that death will not return, and "to take captivity captive" means that captivity will never return, a concept which cannot be expressed through an affirmative assertion.

Chains of the Law hit the ground when the Father calls us sons and daughters.

The old man always chooses slavery. Whether he's bemoaning the shackles of the Law's condemnation or the willing submission to a master who oppresses and abuses, the old man repeatedly walks into captivity. The old man, when hearing the freedom of the Gospel, tries to run away from it, fearing that it's a message that is simply too good to be true.

But when the old man finally runs out of steam and gives up the fight, he is made new by the death of the Son. The One who never could be enslaved by sin or the Law did what the old man never could.

By obedience and sacrifice, Jesus made the old man new and set the prisoner free. He became sin in order to set the captives free. With His death and resurrection, the chains fall and the cellar doors open.

CHAPTER 5

LAW AND GOSPEL

The Christian Church loves this kind of sermon:
Do this.
You're not doing it.
Try harder.

Because of the old man in us, we love a sermon that tells us what we should be doing. If someone gives us orders, we believe that it's up to us to follow those orders; if we're not living up to the demands, we aren't trying hard enough. In the Christian Church, this message is all around us. It's often hidden behind a veil of clever phrases and spiritual language, but the message is ultimately still the same: "Here's what God wants from you. If you're not doing it, just try harder."

The problem with this message is that it's all demands and no comfort. It's all Law and no Gospel. It might be masked with Gospel-sounding encouragement, but however you spin it, "Be better" is always the Law. We hear the commands of God, which might even be accurately communicated in such a sermon, yet when we feel the burden because of our own failures, we are offered no comfort.

And with Christians routinely leaving the Church, I can't help but wonder if maybe the problem is that too many people were part of a church that preached all Law and no Gospel. Maybe people heard a message of "do more" and "try harder" and left exhausted because they did try to do more but never got any better.

David Zahl, Director of Mockingbird Ministries, understood this same problem when he wrote, "Christianity now is in crisis, in large part because people have marketed it as a religion of good people getting better, when in fact it is a religion of bad people coping with their failure to be good."[7]

The proper distinction between Law and Gospel is quite possibly one of the most important emphases in Luther's teaching. It's one that we see developed early on in his writing and one that continues to be repeated in our own day.

This distinction is a matter of life and death.

Preaching the Law to someone who is anguished over sin kicks that person when he's down. And preaching the Gospel to someone who's unrepentant empowers a sinner to live licentiously. But when communicated properly, the Law kills the sinner so that he might be raised to life by the power of the Gospel. The Law diagnoses the sinner so that he might receive the remedy in the death and resurrection of Jesus. The Law exposes the sinner so that the Gospel might expose the Savior.

> For "everyone who calls on the name of the Lord will be saved."
>
> How then will they call on Him in whom they have not believed? And how are they to believe in Him of whom they have never heard? And how are they to hear without someone preaching? And how are they to preach unless they are sent? As it is written, "How beautiful are the feet of those who preach the good news!" (Romans 10:13–15)

MARTIN LUTHER

The preaching of the Gospel is something lovable and desirable for those who are under the Law. For the Law shows nothing but our sin, makes us guilty, and thus produces an anguished conscience; but the Gospel supplies a longed for remedy to people in anguish of this kind. Therefore the Law is evil, and the Gospel good; the Law announces wrath, but the Gospel peace.

The Law oppresses the conscience with sins, but the Gospel frees the conscience and brings peace through faith in Christ.

Thus the feet of the church as it preaches are voices and words by which it cuts and shakes up the people and "beats them to pieces." And the church does this with nothing else than with words and voices. They are "beautiful" and desirable to those whose consciences are pressed down by sins.

---

7   William McDavid, Ethan Richardson, and David Zahl, *Law and Gospel: A Theology for Sinners (and Saints)* (Mockingbird Ministries, 2015), 21.

The Gospel supplies a longed for remedy to people in anguish.

—MARTIN LUTHER

Therefore we have these two sets of contrary terms: Law—sin. The Law shows up sin and makes man guilty and sick; indeed proves him worthy of being damned. Gospel—grace. The Gospel offers grace and remits sin and cures the sickness unto salvation.

God saves no one but sinners, He instructs no one but the foolish and stupid, He enriches none but paupers, and He makes alive only the dead; not those who merely imagine themselves to be such but those who really are this kind of people and admit it.

God saves sinners because that's all that there are. He instructs the foolish because that is all He has to work with. He makes alive the dead because dead people can't make themselves alive. The proper distinction between Law and Gospel makes clear what we do and what we don't do. And it makes clear God does what we don't have the power to do.

> Or do you not know, brothers—for I am speaking to those who know the law—that the law is binding on a person only as long as he lives? For a married woman is bound by law to her husband while he lives, but if her husband dies she is released from the law of marriage. Accordingly, she will be called an adulteress if she lives with another man while her husband is alive. But if her husband dies, she is free from that law, and if she marries another man she is not an adulteress. (Romans 7:1–3)

It is evident that the apostle is not speaking of the Law in a metaphysical or moral sense, but in a spiritual and theological sense. He is dealing with the Law as it applies to the inner man and the will and not with respect to the works of the outer man. Once we have understood his customary propositions and his bases and principles, all the rest is easy.

The first of these principles is:

Sin and the wrath of God come through the Law. Therefore no one dies to the Law unless he dies also to sin, and whoever dies to sin dies also to the Law. And as soon as a man is free from sin, he is also free from the Law. And when a person becomes a servant of sin, he also becomes a slave of the Law, and while sin rules over him and dominates him, the Law also rules over and dominates him.

The Law brings wrath. When you read the words of condemnation and the accusations, this is the Law. The Law's work is exposing the sinner. The Law does its work so that sinners will come to repentance. Any part of Scripture that demands obedience or perfection or tells us what we must do is the Law. Any part of Scripture that describes our failure to follow the Law is also the Law.

Grace and spiritual righteousness picks a man up and changes him.

The Gospel, on the other hand, brings peace. While the Law brings condemnation and accusation, the Gospel brings pardon and amity. While the Law exposes the sinner, the Gospel exposes the Savior who comes for sinners. Any part of Scripture that points to the work of Christ—His obedience, His perfection, His finished work on the cross—is the Gospel.

This way of speaking is a most effective device against the self-righteous. But human righteousness tries first of all to take away sins and change them and also to preserve man as he is; thus it is not righteousness but hypocrisy.

Therefore the hypocrites with amazing foolishness punish themselves with numerous labors and are zealous in changing their works before they with true humility seek the grace which would change them. In Ephesians 2:10: "For we are His workmanship, created in Christ Jesus for good works," he does not say that good works are created in us. And James 1:18 reads: "that we should be a kind of firstfruits of His creatures."

Therefore with marvelous stupidity and with a monkey-sees-monkey-does attitude do these people act who want to imitate the works of the saints and glory in their fathers and ancestors, as the monks do today.

Being holy they are not holy, being righteous they are not righteous, though they do good works they do nothing good.

The first thing we must do is beseech grace so that a man might be changed in spirit and with glad heart and will desire and do all things, not with servile fear or childish cupidity but with a free and manly heart. And this alone the Spirit accomplishes.

Likewise, my brothers, you also have died to the law through the body of Christ, so that you may belong to another, to Him who has been raised from the dead, in order that we may bear fruit for God. For while we were living in the flesh, our sinful passions, aroused by the law, were at work in our members to bear fruit for death. But now we are released from the law, having died to that which held us captive, so that we serve in the new way of the Spirit and not in the old way of the written code. (Romans 7:4–6)

MARTIN LUTHER

The so-called moral interpretation of Scripture, which more correctly is the spiritual interpretation, deals with nothing but love and the attitude of the heart, with nothing but the love of righteousness and the hatred of iniquity, that is, when we ought to do something or give up doing something. And we must understand that this must be done or omitted with the whole heart, not with fear of punishment in a slavish manner or because of some puerile desire for comfort, but freely and out of love for God, because without the love which has been poured out through the Spirit this is impossible.

First Corinthians 13:2: "If I understand all mysteries and have all knowledge, even if I have all faith, etc., but have not love, I gain nothing." Therefore it clearly follows that the term "written code" [in Romans 7:6] applies to the mysteries, to the whole Gospel, and to every spiritual interpretation of the Scripture. Hence if these people are dead, they are without the Spirit; "for the Spirit gives life, and the written code kills" (2 Corinthians 3:6), but these men have been killed and hence are under the written code.

They are not the best Christians who are the most learned and read the most and abound in many books. Rather they are the best Christians who with a totally free will do those things which the scholars read in the books and teach others to do. In our age it is to be feared, that by the making of many books we develop very learned men but very unlearned Christians.

When the question is asked why the Gospel is called the Word of the Spirit, a spiritual teaching, the Word of grace and a clarification of the words of the ancient law and a knowledge that is hidden in a mystery, the reply is that properly the Gospel teaches where and whence we may obtain grace and love, namely, in Jesus Christ, whom the Law promised and the Gospel reveals.

The Law commands us to have love and Jesus Christ, but the Gospel offers and presents them both to us.

God's Law and Gospel are both necessary. They function in different ways, yet work together. The Law commands us to do what we cannot do. The Law demands perfection in obedience. And

The **Law** commands us to have love and **Jesus** **Christ**, but the **Gospel** offers and presents them both to us.

—MARTIN LUTHER

because of the demands, it reveals our sin and accuses us in our failure.

This is bad news.

But there is good news about the bad news. The Law never exists for the sake of itself. The end of the Law is never the Law. The Law always exists for the sake of the Gospel.

Like the Law, the Gospel is also necessary; unlike the Law, the Gospel doesn't make any demands. The Gospel makes only promises. The Gospel promises that we are given everything we need in the death and resurrection of Jesus. The Gospel promises that our sins are forgiven freely—not by our own obedience but by the perfect obedience of Jesus.

The Good News is the last word. The Good News is the word that declares you to be a forgiven and baptized child of God, purchased and won by the blood of Jesus.

Both Law and Gospel are necessary, but they are needed for different reasons.

MARTIN LUTHER

Properly speaking it is Gospel when it preaches Christ; but when it rebukes and reproves and gives commands, it does nothing else than to destroy those who are presumptuous concerning their own righteousness to make room for grace, that they may know that the Law is fulfilled not by their own powers but only through Christ, who pours out the Holy Spirit in our hearts.

They who interpret the term "Gospel" as something else than "the good news" do not understand the Gospel, as those people do who have turned the Gospel into a law rather than grace and have made Christ a Moses[8] for us.

What shall we say, then? That Gentiles who did not pursue righteousness have attained it, that is, a righteousness that is by faith; but that Israel who pursued a law that would lead to righteousness did not succeed in reaching that law. Why? Because they did not pursue it by faith, but as if it were based on works. They have stumbled over the stumbling stone, as it is written, "Behold, I am laying in Zion a stone of stumbling, and a rock of offense; and whoever believes in Him will not be put to shame." (Romans 9:30–33)

---

8 Moses represents the Law because he is the mediator that delivered the Ten Commandments. Those people who turn Christ into a new Moses say that He is simply the giver of a new and improved Law.

The word of the Law was a carnally understood word, imperfect and extended, or prolonged, so the Word of the Spirit, that is, of the Law spiritually understood, is a finished and abbreviated Word.

It was an imperfect word because it signified but did not demonstrate that which it signified. And for this reason it was extended and prolonged, because it led more and more to the imperfect and the carnal, since it was impossible for it to exhibit what was spiritual as long as it was considered and understood in a carnal way.

Just as in the case of a sign, as long as it is accepted in the place of the thing signified, the thing signified is not possessed. And thus in the end this word does not lead "to righteousness" but rather to wickedness, lying and vanity.

On the other hand, the Word of the Gospel is finished, because it bestows what it signifies, namely, grace. It does not defer what it signifies, indeed it actually cuts itself off from all things which prolong and impede the reception of it.

He who believes in Christ will not be in a hurry, will not flee, will not be terrified, for he fears nothing, he stands quiet and secure, established on the solid rock.

Law and Gospel function differently but work in tandem so that sinners will recognize their sin and cling to their Savior. Without the Law, we are unaware of our failure to be righteous before God. The Law tells us what to do by revealing God's will to us, and it makes us come face-to-face with our sin. Without the Gospel, the Law is just bad news. The Gospel allows us to rest because the work is finished. The Gospel proclaims "it is finished" in a world that proclaims "do more." Both of these words are absolutely necessary—to lose one is to also lose the other.

THE BAD NEWS

○ Life with two toddler children means that our days are filled with tantrums, dress-up, and of course, the inevitable scraped knee. Have you ever noticed the miracle-working powers of moms when it comes to scraped knees? Occasionally, my kids will come to me for comfort after incurring scrapes and bruises, but my wife has another level of supernatural gifts when it comes to the kiss that can heal any scrape.

What is it about being a child that makes us believe our mom's kiss can fix any scraped knee?

When it comes to Law and Gospel, we are often children who treat the Law like a mother's magical kiss. When we experience the pain of realizing we are worse than we thought, we try to use the Law as the solution to the problem. We look for the Law to tell us what to do. And often, magically, our own efforts will temporarily make us feel like things are getting better.

Here's the bad news: the Law doesn't actually solve the problem—it only exposes the problem. And trying harder, though necessary, doesn't solve the problem either. In fact, trying harder often just makes us realize how big the problem really is.

This might be frustrating, but when we understand the purpose of the Law, it's okay. The Law isn't meant to heal; it's meant to diagnose the problem. The Law isn't meant to eliminate the disease; it's meant to make you aware of the disease.

The Law doesn't make us better. It makes us turn to the One who can.

The Law isn't the kiss from mom that makes us imagine the pain has gone away; the Law is the surgeon who carefully makes the first incision so there can be healing. The Law is the doctor who diagnoses the disease and prescribes the remedy. The Law is the artist who cuts, hammers, and chisels away in order to create something new.

The Law cuts to the heart of the issue and kills any cancerous belief that thinks our salvation depends on our own efforts. The Law kills us, which sounds bad but is actually good, because God is in the resurrection business. The goal of the Law is to expose us so that we might cry out, "Lord, have mercy."

And in that desperate moment, when we have been cut to the heart with nowhere to turn, the Gospel breathes new life into us. In that moment, when we've been told the clear diagnosis and have received the Gospel remedy, we are given hope in Christ alone. Only when we hear the bad news that makes us cry out, "Lord, have mercy," are we able to hear the Good News of "it is finished."

MARTIN LUTHER

"Through the Law comes the knowledge of sin" [Romans 3:20]. This knowledge through the Law comes in two ways, first, through contemplation, . . . second, through experience, that is, through the work of the Law . . . then man understands how deeply sin and evil are rooted in him.

The "works of the Law" are one thing and the "fulfilling of the Law" another. For grace is the fulfilling of the Law, but not works. Blessed Augustine in the 13th chapter of his *On the Spirit and the Letter* says: "What the law of works commands by its threats, this the law of faith accomplishes by believing. . . . By the law of faith we can say to God in humble prayer: 'Give me what Thou commandest.' For the Law commands in such a way that it tells faith what to do (that is, what it ought to do), in other words, so that if the one who is commanded cannot as yet fulfill the command, he may know what he should ask."

And in chapter 19 Augustine says: " . . . That the Law is not fulfilled is not the fault of the Law, but it is the fault of the thinking of the flesh. This fault had to be shown by the Law but had to be cleansed by grace."

But now the righteousness of God has been manifested apart from the law, although the Law and the Prophets bear witness to it—the righteousness of God through faith in Jesus

Christ for all who believe. For there is no distinction: for all have sinned and fall short of the glory of God, and are justified by His grace as a gift, through the redemption that is in Christ Jesus, whom God put forward as a propitiation by His blood, to be received by faith. This was to show God's righteousness, because in His divine forbearance He had passed over former sins. It was to show His righteousness at the present time, so that He might be just and the justifier of the one who has faith in Jesus.

Then what becomes of our boasting? It is excluded. By what kind of law? By a law of works? No, but by the law of faith. For we hold that one is justified by faith apart from works of the law. Or is God the God of Jews only? Is He not the God of Gentiles also? Yes, of Gentiles also, since God is one—who will justify the circumcised by faith and the uncircumcised through faith. Do we then overthrow the law by this faith? By no means! On the contrary, we uphold the law. (Romans 3:21–31)

Righteousness must be left to Christ alone, and to Him alone the works of grace and of the Spirit.

If we examine ourselves carefully, therefore, we shall always find in ourselves at least vestiges of the flesh by which we are afflicted with self-interest, obstinate over against the good, and prone to do evil. For if there were not this kind of remnant of sin in us and if we were seeking only God, surely this mortal man would quickly be dissolved, and our soul would fly to God. But the fact that the soul does not take to flight is a sure sign that it still clings to the filth of the flesh until it may be freed by the grace of God, and this is to be awaited in death.

It is easy, if we use any diligence at all, to see the depravity of our will in our love of sensual evils and our flight from things that are good. We are drawn toward lust, greed, gluttony, arrogance, love of honor, and we abhor chastity, generosity, sobriety, humility, shame; but it is easy, I say, to understand how in these things we seek our fulfillment and love ourselves, how we are turned in upon ourselves and become ingrown at least in our heart, even when we cannot sense it in our actions.

Any sliver of honesty in us will prompt us to realize sin is a problem that affects us deeply. The Law holds the mirror up to our lives and reveals all the flaws. It points out our idolatry and our pride. It shows us the hypocrisy we've tried to cover up and the gossip we've tried to keep quiet. It even reveals the embarrassing lying, cheating, and manipulating we hoped no one would notice.

Thus we pray, "Forgive us our debts" (Matthew 6:12).

Who, therefore, can exalt himself against another person as if he were more righteous than the other? When he not only can do the same as the other man does, but also in his heart actually does the same before God as the other man does before men. Therefore no one should ever despise a man who sins, but one should kindly help him as one who shares a common misery.

Grace and forbearance are not given in order that we may sin or act as we want to. . . . [God] does not remit sins in such a way that He no longer regards the work of anyone as sin and simply takes the Law away, but He does not punish the sins of the past which He has patiently endured, in order that He may justify. He therefore is not indulgent toward us in order that we may do as we please.

There is a difference, therefore, between sinners and sinners. Some are sinners and confess that they have sinned, but they do not desire to be made righteous; instead, they despair and keep on sinning, so that in death they despair and in life they are slaves to the world.

Notice that statement: "They are slaves to the world."

When our forgiveness leads to a life of sinning, we've actually given up freedom and walked back into the chains of slavery. Freedom doesn't lead the Christian to lawlessness—it simply leads the Christian to see the Law for what it's worth and nothing more. The Law reveals God's will for us to live as Christians but plays no part in our standing before God or in our ability to do what it demands.

Others, however, are sinners and confess that they sin and have sinned, but they grieve about it and hate themselves for it and desire to be made righteous and constantly pray and cry to God for righteousness. These are the people of God, who bear the judgment of the cross like a yoke upon their shoulders.

In the same way there is also a difference between the righteous and the righteous. For some affirm that they are righteous and do not care to be justified, but rather they expect to be rewarded and crowned as kings. Others deny that they are righteous and fear condemnation and desire to be justified.

No one should ever despise a man who sins, but one should help him as kindly as one who shares a common misery.

— MARTIN LUTHER

The devil, therefore, that master of a thousand tricks, lays traps for us with marvelous cleverness.

He leads some astray by getting them involved in open sins.

Others, who think themselves righteous, he brings to a stop, makes them lukewarm, and prompts them to give up the desire for righteousness.

A third group he seduces into superstitions and ascetic sects, so that, for example, in their greater degree of holiness and in their imagined possession of righteousness, they do not at all grow cold but feverishly engage in works, setting themselves apart from the others, whom they despise in their pride and disdain.

A fourth class of people he urges on with ridiculous labor to the point where they try to be completely pure and holy, without any taint of sin. And as long as they realize that they are sinning and that evil may overwhelm them, he so frightens them with the judgment and wears out their consciences that they all but despair.

He senses the weakness of each individual and attacks him in this area. And because these four classes of people are so fervent for righteousness, it is not easy to persuade them to the contrary.

The devil knows exactly what he's doing.

He is the master archnemesis who strategically attacks us where he knows we are most vulnerable. He is the master manipulator of the Law, twisting it to meet his own ends, repeatedly leaving us in a place of despair. When we have been crushed by our own failure, the devil twists the Law by turning up the volume of our despair so that the hope of the Gospel is drowned out. In our own striving toward righteousness, the devil will twist the Law so that we give up on our desire for obedience and our disdain toward sin. And in our own lifestyle, the devil will twist the Law so that it becomes attainable—a place for us to find our identity, finding a false security in our own obedience instead of the perfect obedience of Christ.

[The devil] begins by helping [these four classes of people] to achieve their goal, so that they become overanxious to rid themselves of every evil desire. And when they cannot accomplish this, he causes them to become sad, dejected, wavering, hopeless, and unsettled in their consciences.

Then it only remains for us to stay in our sins and to cry in hope of the mercy of God that He would deliver us from them. Just as the patient who is too anxious to recover can surely have a serious relapse, we must also be healed gradually and for a while put up with certain weaknesses.

For it is sufficient that our sin displeases us, even though we do not get entirely rid of it. For Christ carries all sins, if only they are displeasing to us, and thus they are no longer ours but His, and His righteousness in turn is ours.

> There is therefore now no condemnation for those who are in Christ Jesus. For the law of the Spirit of life has set you free in Christ Jesus from the law of sin and death. For God has done what the law, weakened by the flesh, could not do. By sending His own Son in the likeness of sinful flesh and for sin, He condemned sin in the flesh, in order that the righteous requirement of the law might be fulfilled in us, who walk not according to the flesh but according to the Spirit. For those who live according to the flesh set their minds on the things of the flesh, but those who live according to the Spirit set their minds on the things of the Spirit. For to set the mind on the flesh is death, but to set the mind on the Spirit is life and peace. For the mind that is set on the flesh is hostile to God, for it does not submit to God's law; indeed, it cannot. Those who are in the flesh cannot please God.
>
> You, however, are not in the flesh but in the Spirit, if in fact the Spirit of God dwells in you. Anyone who does not have the Spirit of Christ does not belong to Him. But if Christ is in you, although the body is dead because of sin, the Spirit is life because of righteousness. If the Spirit of Him who raised Jesus from the dead dwells in you, He who raised Christ Jesus from the dead will also give life to your mortal bodies through His Spirit who dwells in you. (Romans 8:1–11)

It is simply impossible for us of ourselves to fulfill the Law, and [it] is of no value to say that we can fulfill the Law.

> At some point, many of us have believed that our own efforts can fix things. Self-justification is simply the way life works. Did I say something to my wife I shouldn't have? If I justify my actions, we'll be good. Did I fail to turn in my homework on time? My self-justification can solve that problem. Did I lie to my best friend? Maybe if I can find the right excuse, my friend will think my lie was justified.
>
> When it comes to fulfilling the Law, we believe either that we are good enough or that our failures are justified.

Both of these are the result of a low view of the Law. Because of the unbearable burden of the Law, Christians have opted for lowering the bar of the Law. After all, if the Law is unattainable, God certainly couldn't have meant what He said.

We take the burden of the Law and make ourselves feel better by saying, "What God really wants is our good intentions." The problem is the Law never works like this in the Scriptures. The Law always accuses and always leaves us crushed by its weight.

We find ourselves with the frustrating realization that we aren't good enough and that no efforts of self-justification will save us. That's what the Law does. And that's what the Law is supposed to do. The Law doesn't make us better. The Law doesn't fix the problem. The Law makes us aware of our problem in order to point us to the One who remedies the problem.

Blessed Augustine says in regard to [Romans 8:3]: "The Law was weakened in that it did not provide the fulfillment for what it commanded, not by its own fault but 'by the flesh,' that is, through men who in seeking after carnal good did not love the righteousness of the Law but preferred temporal pleasures to it."[9]

The expression "the Law was weak" must be referred to the heart or the disposition rather than to an outward work. For people do indeed observe the Law outwardly, but inwardly in the heart they hate it, as we read in the psalm: "Who speak peace with their neighbor, while mischief is in their hearts" (Psalm 28:3).

The apostle prefers to say, "what the Law could not do" rather than "what we could not do," even though this disability belongs to no one but to us, who were weak or unable to fulfill the Law. But he does this in keeping with his practice and because the occasion requires it. For he is arguing primarily against those who trust in the powers of their own nature and think that no other help is necessary for righteousness.

This crookedness, this depravity, this iniquity is condemned over and over in Scripture under the name of fornication and idolatry, and it is . . . something most profound in our nature, indeed, it is our very nature itself, wounded and totally in ferment, so that without grace it becomes not only incurable but also totally unrecognizable.

"Blessed are those whose lawless deeds are forgiven, and whose sins are covered; blessed is the man against whom the

---

9   Augustine, *Expositio quarundem propositionum ex epistula ad Romanos*, 48, *Patrologia, Series Latina*, XXXV, 7072.

Lord will not count his sin." Is this blessing then only for the circumcised, or also for the uncircumcised? For we say that faith was counted to Abraham as righteousness. How then was it counted to him? Was it before or after he had been circumcised? It was not after, but before he was circumcised. He received the sign of circumcision as a seal of the righteousness that he had by faith while he was still uncircumcised. The purpose was to make him the father of all who believe without being circumcised, so that righteousness would be counted to them as well, and to make him the father of the circumcised who are not merely circumcised but who also walk in the footsteps of the faith that our father Abraham had before he was circumcised. (Romans 4:7–12)

O fools, O pig-theologians (*Sawtheologen*)! By your line of reasoning grace was not necessary except because of some new demand above and beyond the Law. For if the Law can be fulfilled by our powers, as they say, then grace is not necessary for the fulfilling of the Law, but only for the fulfilling of some new exaction imposed by God above the Law. Who can endure these sacrilegious notions? When the apostle says that "the Law works wrath" (v. 15) and that the Law "was weakened by the flesh" (Romans 8:3), it certainly cannot be fulfilled without grace.

They could have been made aware of their own foolishness and brought to shame and repentance even by their own experience. For willy-nilly they recognize the evil lusts in themselves. For this reason I say: "Hah! Get busy now, I beg you. Be men! Work with all your might, so that these lusts may no longer be in you. Prove that it is possible by nature to love God, as you say, 'with all your strength' (Luke 10:27) and without any grace. If you are without concupiscence, we will believe you."

All of these monstrosities have come from the fact that they did not know what sin is nor forgiveness. For they reduced sin to some very minute activity of the soul, and the same was true of righteousness.

This life, then, is a life of being healed from sin, it is not a life of sinlessness, with the cure completed and perfect health attained. The church is the inn and the infirmary for those who are sick and in need of being made well. But heaven is the palace of the healthy and the righteous.

The church is the inn and the infirmary for those who are sick and in need of being made well.

—MARTIN LUTHER

Our theologians, however, have deflected the discussion of sin to the matter of good works only and have undertaken to teach only those things by which works might be safeguarded but not how through much agony men should humbly seek healing grace and confess themselves to be sinners. Thus of necessity they make men proud and cause them to think that they are already entirely righteous when they have performed certain outward works. And thus they are not at all concerned about declaring war on their evil lusts through unceasing prayer to the Lord. And the result is that there is now in the church a great deal of falling away after confession.

And this insanity now rages everywhere in the pulpits of those who should be preaching the Word of God.

Therefore [Paul] says in the first place, "blessed (that is, it goes well with him) is he who is made free," that is, who through grace is made free from the burden of his offense, that is, of the sin which he has actually committed. But this is not enough, unless at the same time he "is covered in regard to his sin," that is, his root evil is not imputed to him as sin.

For it is covered when it is still there but not seen, not observed, and not reckoned. That he is freed, rather, that he is made free, means that he is freed not by his own powers, but by God, who acts while he is merely passive himself. For he does not say: "Blessed is he who frees himself by his own merits," but, "he who is freed."

It is foolish and absurd to say: God has obligated us to possess grace and thus to the impossible.

He has not done this. He has not obligated us to possess grace, but He has obligated us to fulfill the Law, in order that He might give this grace to those of us who have been humbled and who implore His grace.

Grace is not an obligation; it is a gift. We have no active role in our possession of grace; we are completely passive. The only thing we offer to God is the sin that makes grace necessary.

When we begin to understand our inability to fulfill the Law, one of the most common temptations is to soften the blow. We try to rewrite the Law in order to make it more attainable.

A command like "Be perfect, as your heavenly Father is perfect" (Matthew 5:48) couldn't mean that we are obligated to perfection. So we reinterpret it and lower the bar to mean that Jesus really just wants us to all try really hard to be good.

Do you see the problem with that?

That's not what Jesus actually taught. When we lower the bar of the Law, we try to make it attainable so that we might not actually need to deal with the reality that we don't do what the Law demands.

But that's the point of the Law. The Law is unattainable because of our sin. Our nature is so corrupt that we will not be able to leap over the bar of the Law. This is precisely why Jesus is necessary. The One who made the Law came so that He might perfectly keep the Law for the people who fail to do what the Law demands.

This is how the Law works.

The fools do not realize that the will, if it were permitted, would never do what the Law prescribes. For the will is hostile toward the good and prone toward evil. This they certainly experience in their own lives, and yet they speak so impiously and sacrilegiously. For as long as the will is hostile toward the Law, it is turned away from the Law and thus does not fulfill it. Therefore there is need for grace, which makes it willing and even glad to obey the Law.

Therefore, I was correct when I said that all our good is outside of us, and this good is Christ, as the apostle says (1 Corinthians 1:30): "God made Him our wisdom, our righteousness, and sanctification, and redemption." And none of these things are in us except through faith and hope in Him.

> For the promise to Abraham and his offspring that he would be heir of the world did not come through the law but through the righteousness of faith. For if it is the adherents of the law who are to be the heirs, faith is null and the promise is void. For the law brings wrath, but where there is no law there is no transgression. (Romans 4:13–15)

Again [the apostle] proves that righteousness does not come from the Law but from faith, according to the fruit and merit of both. For the Law and faith deserve opposite things. That is, the Law merits wrath and the loss of the promise, but faith deserves grace and the fulfillment of the promise, as if to say, if you do not believe the Scripture and its example, at least believe your own experience.

The Law works wrath, that is, when it is not fulfilled, it shows the wrath of God to those who have failed to provide for its fulfillment. Thus the Law is not evil, but they are evil to whom it was given and to whom it works wrath, but to the others (that is, the believers) it works salvation; actually it is not the Law that works this but grace.

Therefore, if the promise were through the Law, since it works wrath, it would follow that the promise is not a promise, but rather a threat.

The Law, as long as it is without faith which fulfills it, makes all people sinners and establishes the fact that they are guilty and thus unworthy of the promise, indeed worthy of wrath and desolation, and in consequence it turns the promise into a threat. For he who has the Law without faith and grace will assuredly see that he is a sinner and worthy of wrath and that therefore he is deprived of the promise.

The Law is an important and powerful word, but it is never the last word. The Law crushes and burdens the sinner, but it's always for the sake of the word that follows. Without the Law, we would never behold the wonder and beauty of the grace that sets us free from its bondage.

CHAPTER 7

THE POWER AND PRIMACY OF THE GOSPEL

In 1537, a reformer by the name of Philip Melanchthon wrote a document to confront the religious and political power in Rome during the Middle Ages. Melanchthon understood that the power of the pope—who claimed to be a divinely appointed mediator between God and man—was a threat to the Gospel.

In Melanchthon's "Treatise on the Power and Primacy of the Pope," he boldly wrote, "The marks of Antichrist plainly agree with the kingdom of the pope and his followers. . . . This being the case, all Christians should beware of participating in the godless doctrine, blasphemies, and unjust cruelty of the pope."[10] The challenge of Melanchthon remains in our day—Christians are called not to cave to the religious institutions that threaten the message of grace.

This doesn't mean that the Law is bad. It's the abuse and misuse of the Law in the Church that's bad. And it's not only bad but also widespread. Christians are fleeing from churches because they've become victims of an abusive, graceless system. Under the facade of biblical teaching, preachers have found a way to inflate their egos by beating up those already wounded by their sin.

The Law is a powerful word. The Law has the power to kill. The Law has the power to condemn and break down. The Law has the power to crush. And all of those powers are necessary—without the power of the Law, we'd never bear witness to the power of the Gospel.

---

10 "The Power and Primacy of the Pope," 39, 41.

But, again, for what end does the Law exist? The Law exposes us so that we might find the remedy in the person and work of Jesus. The Law exposes us so that Jesus' death and resurrection might set us free from sin, death, and the power of the devil.

But instead of being brought to life and set free, people are walking out of churches bloodied, bruised, and crushed by the weight of an impossible to-do list and the repeated exhortation to "just do it."

In his message "The Gospel for Those Broken by the Church,"[11] Dr. Rod Rosenbladt talks about the burden often felt by those who've given up on the Church: "Many times the law has already done its work on them. Boy, has it ever done its work on them! They need more law like they need a hole in the head."

We don't need more churches that use their power to leave people dead in their sins. We need churches that use the power of the Gospel to bring people life.

> Therefore, since we have been justified by faith, we have peace with God through our Lord Jesus Christ. Through Him we have also obtained access by faith into this grace in which we stand, and we rejoice in hope of the glory of God. Not only that, but we rejoice in our sufferings, knowing that suffering produces endurance, and endurance produces character, and character produces hope, and hope does not put us to shame, because God's love has been poured into our hearts through the Holy Spirit who has been given to us. (Romans 5:1–5)

This is the spiritual peace of which all the prophets sing.

The apostle joins together these two expressions, "through Christ" and "by faith," as he did . . . in the expression "since we are justified by faith . . . through our Lord, etc." In the first place, the statement is directed against those who are so presumptuous as to believe that they can approach God without Christ, as if it were sufficient for them to have believed, as if thus by faith alone, but not through Christ, but beside Christ, as if beyond Christ they no longer needed Him after accepting the grace of justification. And now there are many people who from the works of faith make for themselves works of the Law and of the letter.

The hypocrites and legalists swell up with horrifying pride and think that they are now saved and sufficiently righteous because they believe in Christ, but they are unwilling to be considered unrighteous or regarded as fools. And what is this except the

11 Rod Rosenbladt, "The Gospel for Those Broken by the Church," 1517 The Legacy Project, February 10, 2014, www.1517legacy.com/rodrosenbladt/2014/02/the-gospel-for-those-bro-ken-by-the-church.

MARTIN LUTHER

rejection of Christ's protection and a desire to approach God only from faith but not through Christ?

The Law is misused not only in the abuse of power, but also when it is put in a position of primacy. The Law has become the primary message of Christianity. The primacy of the Law in the Church is anti-Christ. We don't need more Law-centered churches; we need more cross-centered churches.

The Law itself is not anti-Christ, but a church that focuses only on the Law certainly is. When churches make the preaching of the Law the primary message, they rob people of grace freely given. When the message is about what you need to do, you miss what Jesus does for you.

A quick survey of the most popular books, studies, and podcasts within Christianity will reveal a repeated message of "do more" and "try harder." Preachers quickly jump to give us the seven steps to better parenting. Writers encourage us to step out in faith and find our dream job. It's not bad to talk about parenting, vocation, or the Christian life—I love to write and preach about all of these. The problem arises when Christianity focuses on the Christian life instead of on Christ.

> Therefore, just as sin came into the world through one man, and death through sin, and so death spread to all men because all sinned—for sin indeed was in the world before the law was given, but sin is not counted where there is no law. Yet death reigned from Adam to Moses, even over those whose sinning was not like the transgression of Adam, who was a type of the one who was to come.

> But the free gift is not like the trespass. For if many died through one man's trespass, much more have the grace of God and the free gift by the grace of that one man Jesus Christ abounded for many. And the free gift is not like the result of that one man's sin. For the judgment following one trespass brought condemnation, but the free gift following many trespasses brought justification. For if, because of one man's trespass, death reigned through that one man, much more will those who receive the abundance of grace and the free gift of righteousness reign in life through the one man Jesus Christ.

> Therefore, as one trespass led to condemnation for all men, so one act of righteousness leads to justification and life for

all men. For as by the one man's disobedience the many were made sinners, so by the one man's obedience the many will be made righteous. Now the law came in to increase the trespass, but where sin increased, grace abounded all the more, so that, as sin reigned in death, grace also might reign through righteousness leading to eternal life through Jesus Christ our Lord. (Romans 5:12–21)

The apostle joins together grace and the gift, as if they were different, but he does so in order that he may clearly demonstrate the type of the One who was to come which he has mentioned, namely, that although we are justified by God and receive His grace, yet we do not receive it by our own merit, but it is His gift.

"Just as Adam has become a cause of death to those who are born of him, even though they have not eaten of the tree, the death brought on by the eating, so also Christ was made a provider of righteousness for those who belong to Him, even though they are entirely lacking in righteousness, and He has given it to us all through His cross."[12]

Thus the likeness of Adam's transgression is in us, because we die, as if we had sinned in the same way he did. And the likeness of Christ's justification is in us, because we live, as if we had produced the same kind of righteousness that He did.

This gift is "by the grace of that one Man," that is, by the personal merit and grace of Christ, by which He was pleasing to God, so that He might give this gift to us. This phrase "by the grace of that one Man" should be understood of the personal grace of Christ, corresponding to the personal sin of Adam which belonged to him, but the "gift" is the very righteousness which has been given to us.

But "the grace of God" and "the gift" are the same thing, namely, the very righteousness which is freely given to us through Christ. And He adds this grace because it is customary to give a gift to one's friends. But this gift is given even to His enemies out of His mercy, because they were not worthy of this gift unless they were made worthy and accounted as such by the mercy and grace of God.

Although often abandoned in the contemporary Christian Church, grace is the primary message of the Church. The Gospel "is the power of God for salvation to everyone who believes" (Romans 1:16). Jesus takes away sin. Jesus' death and resurrection pay the

---

12 Augustine, *Contra Julianum*, I, 6, 22, *Patrologia, Series Latina*, XLIV, 656.

price we couldn't pay. Jesus' perfect obedience fulfills the Law we failed to obey.

Grace is a gift that can't be earned. Jesus' perfect life, death, and resurrection gives us everything we need. He declares us forgiven. He calls us children of God. He sees us as righteous.

Because of sin—which the Law has made us intimately aware of—we could be called enemies of God. But instead, Jesus has "called you friends" (John 15:15).

Notice the beauty of the love and grace found in the work of Jesus:

> I am speaking the truth in Christ—I am not lying; my conscience bears me witness in the Holy Spirit—that I have great sorrow and unceasing anguish in my heart. For I could wish that I myself were accursed and cut off from Christ for the sake of my brothers, my kinsmen according to the flesh. They are Israelites, and to them belong the adoption, the glory, the covenants, the giving of the law, the worship, and the promises. To them belong the patriarchs, and from their race, according to the flesh, is the Christ, who is God over all, blessed forever. Amen. (Romans 9:1–5)

From this text it is very clear that love is found not only in sweetness and delight, but also in the greatest sorrow and bitterness. Indeed it rejoices and delights in bitterness and sorrow, because it regards the misery and sufferings of others as if they were its own. Thus Christ even in the final and worst hour of His suffering was aglow with His deepest love. . . . It filled Him with the greatest joy to suffer the greatest pain.

Christ suffered damnation and desertion more than all the saints. And it was not easy for Him to suffer, as some imagine. For He really and truly offered Himself to God the Father for the condemnation for us. And in His human nature He acted in no way different than a man to be eternally damned to hell. And on account of this love of His toward God, God immediately raised Him from death and hell and thus devoured hell.

> But it is not as though the word of God has failed. For not all who are descended from Israel belong to Israel, and not all are children of Abraham because they are his offspring, but "Through Isaac shall your offspring be named." This means that it is not the children of the flesh who are the children of

Christ even in the final and worst hour of His suffering was aglow with His deepest love.

—MARTIN LUTHER

God, but the children of the promise are counted as offspring. For this is what the promise said: "About this time next year I will return, and Sarah shall have a son." And not only so, but also when Rebekah had conceived children by one man, our forefather Isaac, though they were not yet born and had done nothing either good or bad—in order that God's purpose of election might continue, not because of works but because of Him who calls—she was told, "The older will serve the younger." As it is written, "Jacob I loved, but Esau I hated." (Romans 9:6–13)

It inexorably follows that flesh does not make sons of God and the heirs of the promise, but only the gracious election of God. Thus and only thus the Spirit and grace of God can arise only when the pride of the flesh has been humbled.

Therefore, why does man take pride in his merits and works, which in no way are pleasing to God? For they are good, or meritorious, works, but only because they have been chosen by God from eternity that they please Him. Therefore we do good works only in giving thanks, for the works do not make us good, but our goodness, rather, the goodness of God, makes us good and our works good. For they would not be good in themselves except for the fact that God regards them as good. And they only are, or are not, what He reputes them to be or not to be.

For in this way we conform ourselves to God, who does not regard or consider anything in us as good. And in this way we are already good as long as we recognize nothing as good except God's good and our own good as evil, for he who is wise in this way with God is truly a wise and good man. For he knows that nothing is good outside of God and that in God everything is good.

What shall we say then? Is there injustice on God's part? By no means! For He says to Moses, "I will have mercy on whom I have mercy, and I will have compassion on whom I have compassion." So then it depends not on human will or exertion, but on God, who has mercy. For the Scripture says to Pharaoh, "For this very purpose I have raised you up, that I might show My power in you, and that My name might be proclaimed in all the earth." So then He has mercy on whomever He wills, and He hardens whomever He wills. (Romans 9:14–18)

He seems by these words to be rebuffing those who are anxious and curious about the predestination of themselves or of others, as if to drive them away from thoughts and questions about predestination. As the common saying goes: to whom it comes it comes, and whom it hits it hits.

It is as if He were saying: "No one will know to whom I will be merciful and to whom I will be gracious, nor can anyone be certain about it because of his merits or his works or anything else."

We must note that in the Hebrew the first mentioned expression "I will show mercy" means to be merciful in the sense that He who shows mercy gives a benefit or a free gift even to him who has not offended or committed a sin, but is only in need and poor.

But "I will be [compassionate]," or "I will show mercy," means "to forgive" and "to be gracious," which can take place without benefit for him who is guilty and an offender. As when God remits the penalty of hell and the sin, He shows compassion, but when He gives grace and the kingdom of heaven, He is merciful.

This is not to be understood in the sense that this is a matter only of God's showing mercy, as if it were not necessary for a person to will or to exert himself, but rather that the fact that a man does will or exert himself is not of his own power but of the mercy of God, who has given this power of willing and doing, without which man of himself can neither will nor make exertion.

The apostle says in Philippians 2:13: "God is at work in you, both to will and to work." Here he says the same thing, but in different words: "It depends not upon man's will or exertion," that is, not upon man's doing "but upon God's mercy," that is, upon God who gives the gift of His grace. Thus in Psalm 119:32: "I will run in the way of Thy commandments," that is, I have accomplished something, "when Thou enlargest my understanding," that is, when Thou hast made me to will and to be able.

Jeremiah 10:23 tells us: "I know, O Lord, that the way of man is not in himself, that it is not in a man who walks to direct his steps." In all of these things there is a kind of contradiction.

For if a man's way is not his own, why then does it say: "his way"? The way of man is not his way. So also here: "it depends not on man's exertion," that is, the race he runs, nor does it "depend upon his will," that is, his volition. This is a remarkable thing!

The volition is not his who wills, and the race is not his who runs, but God's, who gives it and creates it.

In the same way the apostle says in Galatians 2:20: "I live, yet not I." And Christ says: "My teaching is not Mine" (John 7:16).

> You will say to me then, "Why does He still find fault? For who can resist His will?" But who are you, O man, to answer back to God? Will what is molded say to its molder, "Why have you made me like this?" Has the potter no right over the clay, to make out of the same lump one vessel for honorable use and another for dishonorable use? What if God, desiring to show His wrath and to make known His power, has endured with much patience vessels of wrath prepared for destruction, in order to make known the riches of His glory for vessels of mercy, which He has prepared beforehand for glory— even us whom He has called, not from the Jews only but also from the Gentiles? As indeed He says in Hosea, "Those who were not My people I will call 'My people,' and her who was not beloved I will call 'beloved.' " "And in the very place where it was said to them, 'You are not My people,' there they will be called 'sons of the living God.' " (Romans 9:19–26)

The question is asked: Is the apostle saying these things with any logical connection to what he has said previously? The answer is that he is speaking in a very orderly way, for he has said previously that all things take place according to God's election. Jacob was loved by God because he had been elected, and he obtained mercy because it thus pleased God from eternity, just as also He said to Moses, "I will show mercy, etc." (Exodus 33:19).

Having made these statements, he immediately and correctly brings in the corollary which obviously follows what has been said, namely, that it is solely because of a merciful God that anyone is chosen or is righteous, inasmuch as all men are equally a part of the mass of perdition and no one is righteous before God unless he receives mercy.

Everything depends on a merciful God and not on someone's will.

It is the same today; in order to humble the elect and to teach them to trust in His mercy alone, to lay aside every presumption of their own will and achievement, God permits them to be desperately afflicted and to be pursued by the devil, the world, or the flesh, whom He Himself arouses against them. And yet through all of these things He leads them out and finally frees them unexpectedly while they in despair groan over the fact that they actually will and do such evil things and do not will and do so many good things which they want.

The primary message of the Church is a message of grace, hope, and love. Paul writes in Romans 1:16, "For I am not ashamed of the gospel, for it is the power of God for salvation to everyone who believes." The Law has power, but it doesn't have the power to save. The Law has influence, but it doesn't truly change our hearts. The Law does a work, but it doesn't do the same work as the Gospel.

It's time that our churches use the powerful Word given to us in order to "proclaim good news to the poor . . . [and] to proclaim liberty to the captives" (Luke 4:18).

The death and resurrection of Jesus gives hope to the hopeless and sets the captives free.

> For I tell you that Christ became a servant to the circumcised to show God's truthfulness, in order to confirm the promises given to the patriarchs, and in order that the Gentiles might glorify God for His mercy. . . . May the God of hope fill you with all joy and peace in believing, so that by the power of the Holy Spirit you may abound in hope. (Romans 15:8–9, 13)

MARTIN LUTHER

What a wonderful title, the "God of hope"! But this is the sign by which the apostle distinguishes between false gods and the true God. For false gods are demons, gods of material things, because they possess those people who in their reliance on material things do not know how to hope. For he who relies on the true God, when all material things have been taken away, lives by pure hope alone.

Therefore the "God of hope" is the same as the God of those who hope. For He is not the God of those who are timorous and despairing, but rather their enemy and their judge. And in short He is the "God of hope" because He is the one who bestows hope. He is that even more because hope alone worships Him, for as He is called "the God of Abraham and Isaac and Jacob" and "the God of Israel," so also He is called "the God of hope," because where there is hope, there He is worshiped.

Sin, death, and the devil have no power that can compare to the power of the Gospel. Because of Jesus, we are no longer slaves to sin; we are sons and daughters of our Father.

The "God of hope" is the God who gives hope when the Law has left us in despair. The grace given to us in the death and resurrection of Jesus gives us the hope and peace of knowing our sins are forgiven. It's a message of hope instead of despair.

With all joy and peace, that is, with a trusting conscience and with mutual concord. He puts joy first and then peace, because joy makes a man peaceful and composed in himself, and when he has become composed, it is easy for him to make peace with others. But he who is sad and disturbed is easily upset at others and of a stormy mind.

But all these things take place *in believing*, because our joy and peace do not consist in something material, but are beyond material things, in hope. Otherwise the God of hope would not give them, for He gives good things which are hidden, joy in sadness and personal affliction, peace in the midst of tumult and outward persecution. Where faith is lacking, a person falls in sadness and persecution, because material things, in which he had placed his trust while they were available, fail him.

The Law is absolutely necessary, but it's not primary. The Law is powerful and helpful, but it never has the power of the Gospel. We are saved by the work of Christ alone. No efforts or intentions, no motivational speeches or self-help gurus will give peace to the troubled consciences. Nothing but the death and resurrection of Jesus will forgive your sins.

That is the message of the Church. It's the message that the Church has historically made primary. And it is this message that resurrects those who are dead in their sins.

CHAPTER 8

RIGHTEOUSNESS

○ In the Sermon on the Mount, Jesus makes a bold statement: "For I tell you, unless your righteousness exceeds that of the scribes and Pharisees, you will never enter the kingdom of heaven" (Matthew 5:20).

In the Scriptures, the Pharisees usually are slammed for their hypocrisy. But that's not what's happening here. In this verse, Jesus is holding them up as an example of good Christian behavior. Because when it comes to good behavior, the Pharisees do it right. They are always on their best behavior; they are the pinnacle of holiness. The apostle Paul at one point refers to his own life as a Pharisee and suggests, "As to righteousness under the law, [I am] blameless" (Philippians 3:6).

How good of a Christian do you have to be in order to call yourself blameless?

When Jesus says, "Unless your righteousness exceeds that of the scribes and Pharisees," He is really saying, "You need to be better than blameless, better than the best of the best." He is indicating that unless you are better than flawless, your good is still inadequate. That creates a problem, doesn't it? What do you do when your best is not good enough?

Jesus is telling you that it doesn't matter how much good you can muster up; doing good doesn't improve your standing before God. You can tithe, you can go to church, and you can share the Gospel with your neighbors—but it doesn't matter how much good you do, for you will still be left short of a right standing with God.

Even the good you have to offer before God doesn't make you right with God. Even the best you have to offer isn't enough.

> But if our unrighteousness serves to show the righteousness of God, what shall we say? That God is unrighteous to inflict wrath on us? (I speak in a human way.) By no means! For then how could God judge the world? But if through my lie God's truth abounds to His glory, why am I still being condemned as a sinner? And why not do evil that good may come?—as some people slanderously charge us with saying. Their condemnation is just. (Romans 3:5–8)

The righteousness of God is not commended because I commit unrighteousness but rather because I confess that I have done unrighteousness and cease to do it, and thus embrace the righteousness of God or what comes from God, since even my righteousness is unrighteousness before Him.

We must speak the same way about truthfulness, for the truthfulness of God is not glorified because I am a liar but because I recognize that I am a liar and cease being one by embracing the truth which comes from God.

Now, what we have said here about truthfulness and lying, righteousness and unrighteousness, must be applied to all other perfections and their opposites, for example, strength and weakness, wisdom and foolishness, innocence and sin, etc. For there is an unending controversy about all of these things between God and proud men . . . for the very reason that they are liars, unrighteous, foolish, weak, sinful men to be made truthful, righteous, wise, strong, innocent men through His truthfulness, righteousness, wisdom, strength, and innocence, and thus to be freed from lying, unrighteousness, foolishness, weakness, and sin, in order that His truthfulness, righteousness, wisdom, strength, and innocence may be glorified and commended in them and by them. Then those haughty people, being men who consider themselves truthful, righteous, wise, strong, and innocent by their own powers and of themselves, refuse and speak against God and thus with all their might judge Him and make Him the liar, the unrighteous, foolish, and weak sinner. For they want to establish their own truthfulness, righteousness, wisdom, virtue, and innocence, and they refuse to be looked upon as liars, unrighteous, foolish, weak sinners. Therefore either God or they must be the liars, the unrighteous, and the weak, etc.

This is like the case of the doctor . . . who wishes to heal his patient, but finds that he is a man who denies that he is sick, calling the doctor a fool and an even sicker person than himself for presuming to cure a healthy man. And because of the man's resistance the doctor cannot get around to recommending his skill and his medicine. For he could do so only if the sick man would admit his illness and permit him to cure him.

Thus these ungodly and arrogant men, although they are sick before God, seem most healthy to themselves. Therefore they not only reject God as their physician, but they even regard Him as a fool and a liar and even sicker than themselves.

Therefore we need humility and faith. What these words seek to establish and maintain is solely this, that inwardly we become nothing, that we empty ourselves of everything, humble ourselves and say with the prophet, "Against Thee, Thee only, have I sinned, so that Thou art justified in Thy words."

And thus to sum up the matter: God is justified in three ways.

First, when He punishes the unrighteous. For then He shows that He is righteous and His righteousness is manifested and commended through the punishment of our unrighteousness. But this is a moderate commendation, because even the ungodly punish the ungodly.

The second way is incidental, or relative, as when opposites which are placed along side each other shine more brightly than when placed by themselves. In the same way the righteousness of God is the more beautiful, the fouler our unrighteousness is. But at this point the apostle is not referring to these ideas, because this is the internal and formal righteousness of God.

Third, when He justifies the ungodly and pours out His grace upon them, or when it is believed that He is righteous in His words. For through such believing He justifies, that is, He accounts people righteous. Hence this is called the righteousness of faith and the righteousness of God.

When I acknowledge that I cannot be righteous before God . . . then I begin to seek my righteousness from Him.

The prophet Isaiah describes the good that we have to offer to God. He writes, "All our righteous deeds are like a polluted garment" (Isaiah 65:6). In other words, even when you do good things, they're still stained with sin. Even when our outward actions are good, there's still the inward, inner battle of the evil that remains within us.

When I acknowledge that I cannot be righteous before God... then I begin to seek my righteousness from Him.

—MARTIN LUTHER

Our best is not good enough.

So, this is why Jesus teaches what He does. And this is what all of the Scriptures point to. If Matthew 5 raises the question "How do we have a righteousness that surpasses that of the Pharisees? How do we have a right standing with God that is better than blameless?" then all of the Scriptures—every letter, phrase, and punctuation mark—point to the same answer: Jesus Christ.

Our best is not good enough. But Christ's is more than enough.

> What then? Are we Jews any better off? No, not at all. For we have already charged that all, both Jews and Greeks, are under sin, as it is written: "None is righteous, no, not one; no one understands; no one seeks for God. All have turned aside; together they have become worthless; no one does good, not even one." (Romans 3:9–12)

The explanation is that those who are manifestly evil sin both according to the inner and the outer man and are without any kind of righteousness, even among themselves. But those who appear outwardly good to themselves and to their fellowmen actually sin in the inner man. For although they do good works outwardly, yet they do them out of fear of punishment or of love for money, glory, or some other material consideration, not willingly and joyfully, and thus the outer man, to be sure, is impelled to good works, but the inner man abounds in concupiscence and contrary lusts. For if he were permitted to act with impunity or if he knew that glory and peace would not come to him, he would rather omit doing good and would do evil, just like the others. Therefore what is the qualitative difference between the man who does evil and the man who wants to do evil, granted that he does not do so because he is compelled by fear or lured by the love of some temporal reward?

The just man whom the apostle is seeking is very rare.

This is the case because we so rarely analyze ourselves deeply enough to recognize this weakness in our will, or rather, this disease. And thus we rarely humble ourselves, rarely seek the grace of God in the right way, for we do not understand, as he says here (v. 11). For this disease is so subtle that it cannot be fully managed even by very spiritual men.

Those who are truly righteous not only sigh and plead for the grace of God because they see that they have an evil inclination and thus are sinful before God, but also because they see that they can never understand fully how deep is the evil of their will and how far it extends, they believe that they are always sinners, as if the depth of their evil will were infinite. Thus they humble themselves, thus they plead, thus they cry, until at last they are perfectly cleansed—which takes place in death.

Just as the statement "There is none righteous" is to be understood of these two classes of man, namely, those who have strayed to the left and those who have strayed to the right, so also we should interpret the expressions "No one understands" and "No one seeks." For because they are not righteous, the former do not understand and do not seek for God because of a lack of interest and negligence; the latter are in the same situation, but because of excess and overdoing.

[The apostle] says, "No one understands," before he says, "No one seeks." For knowing comes before willing and doing; seeking prompts volition and action. But this itself comes after understanding.

Therefore, according to these two classes a man is properly called righteous if he is blessed with understanding and seeks God according to that understanding.

These three statements can be understood as a device whereby we are led from a lesser to a greater expression:

The clause "None is righteous" is the same as the expression "All have turned aside."

The expression "No one understands" is the same as "Together they have gone wrong."

The expression "No one seeks for God" is the same as saying "No one does good."

> As it is written . . . "Their throat is an open grave; they use their tongues to deceive." "The venom of asps is under their lips." "Their mouth is full of curses and bitterness." "Their feet are swift to shed blood; in their paths are ruin and misery, and the way of peace they have not known." "There is no fear of God before their eyes." (Romans 3:10, 13–18)

To criticize a sinner and to castigate him with words is to chew him with the teeth until he is cut into small pieces and made soft (that is, humble and meek). But to flatter and to excuse his sins or to be quick to overlook them, this is to gulp them down the throat, that is, to leave them whole and in large, hard chunks, that is, proud and obdurate toward repentance and unwilling to endure any correction.

Now we know that whatever the law says it speaks to those who are under the law, so that every mouth may be stopped, and the whole world may be held accountable to God. For by works of the law no human being will be justified in His sight, since through the law comes knowledge of sin. (Romans 3:19–20)

The Law asserts that all are unrighteous, so that all because of this assertion may recognize that they are unrighteous and may cease considering themselves righteous and cease boasting, keep silent about their own righteousness, and become guilty in the face of God's righteousness.

The works of the Law are those . . . which take place outside of faith and grace and are done at the urging of the Law, which either forces obedience through fear or allures us through the promise of temporal blessings.

But the works of faith . . . are those which are done out of the spirit of liberty and solely for the love of God.

Brothers, my heart's desire and prayer to God for them is that they may be saved. For I bear them witness that they have a zeal for God, but not according to knowledge. For, being ignorant of the righteousness of God, and seeking to establish their own, they did not submit to God's righteousness. For Christ is the end of the law for righteousness to everyone who believes.

For Moses writes about the righteousness that is based on the law, that the person who does the commandments shall live by them. But the righteousness based on faith says, "Do not say in your heart, 'Who will ascend into heaven?' " (that is, to bring Christ down) "or 'Who will descend into the abyss?' " (that is, to bring Christ up from the dead). But what does it say? "The word is near you, in your mouth and in your heart" (that is, the word of faith that we proclaim). (Romans 10:1–8)

["They have a zeal for God, but not according to knowledge"] is a prodigious statement, because it is the essential and sole opponent of faith, it resists obedience, it makes men stiff-necked and incorrigible. As if it were impossible for them to make a mistake, they stand firm and obstinate in their good intention, staking their entire salvation on the fact that they are carrying out their pious intention out of a zeal for God. Scripture very properly calls these men depraved or crooked in heart and corrupt in mind.

Therefore we must take note that "to have [a zeal for God according to knowledge]" is to be zealous for God in pious ignorance and mental darkness.

The apostle is comparing the two kinds of righteousness with each other. He attributes works to the righteousness of the Law but the Word to the righteousness of faith. For work was required for the Law, but faith is required for the Word. Thus the first kind of righteousness depends on the work which has been done, but the second upon the Word which we believe. And what this Word is he describes when he says, "Do not say in your heart, 'Who will ascend into heaven?' " (v. 6), as if to say that the Word which must be believed is nothing else than this: Christ died and is risen again.

Throughout the Scriptures, we see a distinction in two kinds of righteousness: There is a righteousness that comes solely from the work of Christ, which describes our standing before God. And there is a righteousness that comes in our relationship with our neighbor.

Although the righteousness we have before our neighbor is active (it depends on how we treat our neighbor), the righteousness we have before God is completely passive. It's not our doing; it rests exclusively on the work of Christ. Jesus declared, "It is finished." We are powerless to do what only God can do.

Passive righteousness is the vertical relationship between God and man. God does the work. The only contribution that man brings into this equation is sin. This is a righteousness that is alien; it is completely outside of ourselves.

MARTIN LUTHER

The intent of the apostle is that the total righteousness of man leading to salvation depends on the Word through faith and not on good works through knowledge.

Nothing but faith can accomplish this. For God does not require a magnitude of good works but the mortification of the old man. And he is not mortified except through faith, which humbles our own feeling of self-importance and makes a person subject to that of another.

> If you confess with your mouth that Jesus is Lord and believe in your heart that God raised Him from the dead, you will be saved. For with the heart one believes and is justified, and with the mouth one confesses and is saved. For the Scripture says, "Everyone who believes in Him will not be put to shame." (Romans 10:9–11)

It is as if he were saying: "One does not arrive at righteousness by works, by wisdom, by zeal, but also not by riches and honors," even though many people today promise themselves release from their sins by paying two pennies. And many people want to appear righteous in their own eyes, because they know, read, or teach great things, or because they shine with great dignity and minister in sacred matters.

In the case of the righteousness of God a man is indebted to everyone, for "he is guilty of all of it" (James 2:10). To his Creator, whom he has offended, he owes glory and the blamelessness of his life; to the creation he owes good use and cooperation in the service of God. Therefore he is not able to pay this debt unless he humbles himself in subjection to all of these elements, taking the lowest place, asking nothing for himself among all of these things. As the jurists say: "He who surrenders all his goods has made satisfaction."

The faith which leads to righteousness does not arrive at its goal of righteousness, that is, salvation, if it does not arrive at confession.

> For there is no distinction between Jew and Greek; for the same Lord is Lord of all, bestowing His riches on all who call on Him. For "everyone who calls on the name of the Lord will be saved." (Romans 10:12–13)

God gives to those who call upon Him even more than they request, so that, just as the request in comparison with the gift is poor and modest, so the one who makes the request could not even have contemplated such great gifts. Thus we read in Ephesians 3:20: "He is able to do far more abundantly than all that we ask or think."

God, therefore, is rich as He hears us, but we are poor as we pray; He is powerful in His fulfilling, while we are weak and fearful in our asking. For we do not ask as much as He is willing and able to give, that is, we do not ask according to His power but far beneath His power and in accordance with our own infirmity. But He cannot give except in accord with His power. Therefore He always gives more than is requested.

> How then will they call on Him in whom they have not believed? And how are they to believe in Him of whom they have never heard? And how are they to hear without someone preaching? And how are they to preach unless they are sent? As it is written, "How beautiful are the feet of those

who preach the good news!" But they have not all obeyed the gospel. For Isaiah says, "Lord, who has believed what he has heard from us?" So faith comes from hearing, and hearing through the word of Christ. (Romans 10:14–17)

All people who are of a proud mind [the heretics and schismatics] arrogate to themselves these four qualities in this order. They are all deceived by the appearance of piety. For these four points are so interrelated that the one follows upon the other, and the last is the cause and antecedent of all the others, that is, it is impossible for them to preach unless they are sent; from this it follows that it is impossible for them to hear unless they are preached to; and from this, that it is impossible for them to believe if they do not hear; and then it is impossible for them to call upon God if they do not believe; and finally it is impossible for them to be saved if they do not call upon God. Thus the whole root and origin of our salvation lies in God who sends.

That is why it depends on faith, in order that the promise may rest on grace and be guaranteed to all his offspring—not only to the adherent of the law but also to the one who shares the faith of Abraham, who is the father of us all, as it is written, "I have made you the father of many nations"—in the presence of the God in whom he believed, who gives life to the dead and calls into existence the things that do not exist. In hope he believed against hope, that he should become the father of many nations, as he had been told, "So shall your offspring be." He did not weaken in faith when he considered his own body, which was as good as dead (since he was about a hundred years old), or when he considered the barrenness of Sarah's womb. (Romans 4:16–19)

In the first place, "hope" signifies a thing which is naturally hoped for, but this hope was not of this kind. In the second place, however, it also signifies something which is supernaturally hoped for.

This beautifully suggests the difference between the hope of people generally and the hope of Christians. For the hope of people in general is not contrary to hope but according to hope, that is, what can reasonably be expected to happen. They presume that when certain things have begun, then that which was hoped for will come to pass. And then, finally, they hope that there will be no impediment to prevent what they have hoped for.

The whole whole root and origin of our salvation lies in God who sends.

-MARTIN LUTHER

By contrast, the hope of Christians is certain about the negative aspects. For it knows that the thing hoped for must come to pass and will not be hindered, as long as it is hoped for. For no one can hinder God. But with respect to the positive side, this faith is very unsure, since it has nothing certain in which it can trust, for all things are too hidden, and everything appears contrary. Thus this hope is more positive than negative.

> No unbelief made him waver concerning the promise of God, but he grew strong in his faith as he gave glory to God, fully convinced that God was able to do what he had promised. That is why his faith was "counted to him as righteousness." But the words "it was counted to him" were not written for his sake alone, but for ours also. (Romans 4:20–24)

Just as one glorifies God by believing, so through contrary unbelief he dishonors Him, 1 John 5:10, "He who does not believe in His Son, makes God a liar, because he has not believed in the testimony that God has borne to His Son."

Therefore he who believes God makes God truthful and himself a liar. For he discredits his own feelings as false in order that he might trust in the Word of God as true, which, however, is absolutely contrary to his own feelings.

> It will be counted to us who believe in Him who raised from the dead Jesus our Lord, who was delivered up for our trespasses and raised for our justification. (Romans 4:24–25)

The death of Christ is the death of sin, and His resurrection is the life of righteousness, because through His death He has made satisfaction for sin, and through His resurrection He has brought us righteousness. And thus His death not only signifies but actually effects the remission of sin as a most sufficient satisfaction.

On the cross, Jesus offers Himself to us. When we have nothing to offer but our unrighteousness, God offers His own righteousness. It's not about our sacrifice or our commitment, but it's about His. Our best is not good enough and never will be, but Jesus gives us something to hope in. It's not about our efforts—it's about His.

The theological jargon for this has historically been termed "imputed righteousness." The righteousness of Jesus is imputed to us, declared to be ours by faith. The perfect obedience of the Law is declared to be ours because of the work of Jesus. And our sin—our unrighteousness—is imputed to Jesus.

On the cross, our worst becomes Christ's, and His best becomes ours. On the cross, Jesus becomes the murderer, the adulterer, and the liar. All our sins become His. And by the cross, all that belongs to Christ is offered to us. His holiness and his righteousness become ours.

In a great exchange, we receive all of the righteousness of Jesus and He receives all of our unrighteousness. Because of that exchange, that imputation, Paul writes, "There is therefore now no condemnation for those who are in Christ Jesus" (Romans 8:1). Our unrighteousness never gets the last word, because Jesus' righteousness does.

CHAPTER 9

SINNERS, SAINTS, AND THE SIMUL

One of the central teachings that came about during the time of the Reformation was *simul justus et peccator*, a Latin phrase that refers to the fact that a Christian is at the same time righteous yet sinful. *Simul* is where we get the word *simultaneously*. We are simultaneously justified and sinner. We are both saints and sinners at the same time. We are sick and healed. We are guilty and forgiven. (Once you know a few Latin phrases, you can officially impress your friends with your theological prowess.) Although Luther lectured on Romans well before the recognized start of the Reformation, it is evident that he already had a great understanding of the tension between the old man and the new man that is described by these words before this phrase became popular.

The Christian life is found in this tension. Are we sinners or saints? The tension understands that we are saints, yet a war still rages on as our old self fights against the new. The tension embraces the fact that on one hand we are completely unrighteous, yet on the other hand we are completely righteous.

Embrace the tension.

This is why Paul writes in Romans, "I do not do what I want" (7:15). He understands that the sinner in him is constantly in tension with the saint in him. He is guided by the Spirit and looks outward with love for others, yet he is guided simultaneously by his sinful nature and looks inward at what would be best for himself.

On the one hand, we are completely unrighteous. Romans 3:10–12 says, "None is righteous, no, not one; no one understands; no one seeks for God. All have turned aside; together they have become worthless; no one does good, not even one."

But on the other hand, we are completely righteous because of the work of Christ. Romans 3 also says that this righteousness is given through faith in Jesus Christ to all who believe. "There is no distinction: for all have sinned and fall short of the glory of God, and are justified by His grace as a gift, through the redemption that is in Christ Jesus" (vv. 22–24).

Sinner and saint.

Both at the same time.

> What then shall we say was gained by Abraham, our forefather according to the flesh? For if Abraham was justified by works, he has something to boast about, but not before God. For what does the Scripture say? "Abraham believed God, and it was counted to him as righteousness." Now to the one who works, his wages are not counted as a gift but as his due. And to the one who does not work but believes in him who justifies the ungodly, his faith is counted as righteousness, just as David also speaks of the blessing of the one to whom God counts righteousness apart from works: "Blessed are those whose lawless deeds are forgiven, and whose sins are covered; blessed is the man against whom the Lord will not count his sin." (Romans 4:1–8)

The saints are always sinners in their own sight, and therefore always justified outwardly.

But the hypocrites are always righteous in their own sight, and thus always sinners outwardly.

I use the term "inwardly" to show how we are in ourselves, in our own eyes, in our own estimation; and the term "outwardly" to indicate how we are before God and in His reckoning. Therefore we are righteous outwardly when we are righteous solely by the imputation of God and not of ourselves or of our own works. For His imputation is not ours by reason of anything in us or in our own power. Thus our righteousness is not something in us or in our power.

For if we are righteous only because God reckons us to be such, then it is not because of our mode of living or our deeds. Thus inwardly . . . we are always unrighteous. Thus we read in Psalm 51:3–4, "My sin is ever before me," that is, I always have it in my

Wonderful and sweet is the mercy of God who at the same time considers us both as sinners and nonsinners.

—MARTIN LUTHER

mind that I am a sinner.

Therefore, wonderful and sweet is the mercy of God, who at the same time considers us both as sinners and nonsinners. Sin remains and at the same time it does not remain.

This is the basis for the statement (1 John 1:8): "If we say we have no sin, we are liars." And the mistake lies in thinking that this evil can be cured through works, since experience bears witness that in whatever good work we perform, this concupiscence toward evil remains, and no one is ever cleansed of it, not even the one-day-old infant.

But the mercy of God is that this does remain and yet is not imputed as sin to those who call upon Him and cry out for His deliverance. Thus in ourselves we are sinners, and yet through faith we are righteous by God's imputation. For we believe Him who promises to free us, and in the meantime we strive that sin may not rule over us but that we may withstand it until He takes it from us.

It is similar to the case of a sick man who believes the doctor who promises him a sure recovery and in the meantime obeys the doctor's order in the hope of the promised recovery and abstains from those things which have been forbidden him, so that he may in no way hinder the promised return to health or increase his sickness until the doctor can fulfill his promise to him.

Now is this sick man well?

The fact is that he is both sick and well at the same time. He is sick in fact, but he is well because of the sure promise of the doctor, whom he trusts and who has reckoned him as already cured, because he is sure that he will cure him; for he has already begun to cure him and no longer reckons to him a sickness unto death.

In the same way Christ, our Samaritan, has brought His half-dead man into the inn to be cared for, and He has begun to heal him, having promised him the most complete cure unto eternal life, and He does not impute his sins, that is, his wicked desires, unto death, but in the meantime in the hope of the promised recovery He prohibits him from doing or omitting things by which his cure might be impeded and his sin, that is, his concupiscence, might be increased.

Now, is he perfectly righteous?

No, for he is at the same time both a sinner and a righteous man; a sinner in fact, but a righteous man by the sure imputation and promise of God that He will continue to deliver him from sin until He has completely cured him. And thus he is entirely healthy in hope, but in fact he is still a sinner; but he has the beginning of righteousness, so that he continues more and more always to seek it, yet he realizes that he is always unrighteous. But now if this sick man should like his sickness and refuse every cure for his disease, will he not die? Certainly, for thus it is with those who follow their lusts in this world. Or if a certain sick man does not see that he is sick but thinks he is well and thus rejects the doctor, this is the kind of operation that wants to be justified and made well by its own works.

We are righteous not by our own doing but by the work of Jesus. Yet at the same time we are sinners. We are delivered from sin yet corrupted by sin. We are dead in our trespasses yet alive in Christ. We are plagued by the old man, yet given new life in the new man.

The tension in the *simul* is that we are completely and fully righteous on account of Christ, yet in this life, the old man still fights against the new man. We are not partially righteous—as though the rest of our righteousness depends on us and our own efforts. We are in good standing with our heavenly Father solely by the work of Jesus. But the sinner in us calls us back to the life that Christ called us out of. The sinner in us drags us back into the muck and the mire that Christ pulled us out of.

I am a forgiven, baptized child of God. I am a saint. But I'm also a sinner.

> What then shall we say? That the law is sin? By no means! Yet if it had not been for the law, I would not have known sin. For I would not have known what it is to covet if the law had not said, "You shall not covet." But sin, seizing an opportunity through the commandment, produced in me all kinds of covetousness. For apart from the law, sin lies dead. I was once alive apart from the law, but when the commandment came, sin came alive and I died. The very commandment that promised life proved to be death to me. For sin, seizing an opportunity through the commandment, deceived me and through it killed me. So the law is holy, and the commandment is holy and righteous and good.
>
> Did that which is good, then, bring death to me? By no means! It was sin, producing death in me through what is good, in order that sin might be shown to be sin, and through the commandment might become sinful beyond measure. For we know that the law is spiritual, but I am of the flesh, sold under sin. (Romans 7:7–14)

This entire passage clearly indicates a complaint and a hatred of the flesh and a love for the good and for the Law. But this attitude is in no way characteristic of carnal man, who prefers to hate the Law and laughs at it and follows the desires of his flesh. For the spiritual man fights with his flesh and groans because he cannot do as he wants to. But the carnal man does not fight against his flesh, but yields to it and consents to it.

It is characteristic of a spiritual and wise man to know that he is carnal and displeasing to himself, to hate himself and to approve the law of God because it is spiritual. On the other hand, it is characteristic of a foolish and carnal man to know that he is spiritual, to be well pleased with himself, and to love his life in this world.

> For I do not understand my own actions. For I do not do what I want, but I do the very thing I hate. Now if I do what I do not want, I agree with the law, that it is good. So now it is no longer I who do it, but sin that dwells within me. For I know that nothing good dwells in me, that is, in my flesh. For I have the desire to do what is right, but not the ability to carry it out. For I do not do the good I want, but the evil I do not want is what I keep on doing. Now if I do what I do not want, it is no longer I who do it, but sin that dwells within me.
>
> So I find it to be a law that when I want to do right, evil lies close at hand. For I delight in the law of God, in my inner being, but I see in my members another law waging war against the law of my mind and making me captive to the law of sin that dwells in my members. Wretched man that I am! Who will deliver me from this body of death? Thanks be to God through Jesus Christ our Lord! So then, I myself serve the law of God with my mind, but with my flesh I serve the law of sin. (Romans 7:15–25)

We must not think that the apostle wants to be understood as saying that he does the evil which he hates, and does not do the good which he wants to, in a moral or metaphysical sense, as if he did nothing good but only evil; for in common parlance this might seem to be the meaning of his words. But he is trying to say that he does not do the good as often and as much and with as much ease as he would like. For he wants to act in a completely pure, free, and joyful manner, without being troubled by his rebellious flesh, and this he cannot accomplish.

It is as with a man who proposes to be chaste; he would wish not to be attacked by temptations and to possess his chastity with complete ease. But his flesh does not allow him, for with its drives and inclinations it makes chastity a very heavy burden, and it arouses unclean desires, even though his spirit is unwilling. He who proposes to watch, to pray, and to help his neighbor will always find that his flesh is rebellious and that it devises and desires other things.

For I know that nothing good dwells within me, that is, in my flesh. (v. 18). See how he attributes to himself flesh which is a part of him as if he himself were flesh. Because of his flesh he is carnal and wicked, for there is no good in him, and he does evil; because of the spirit he is spiritual and good, because he does good.

Because the same one complete man consists of flesh and spirit, therefore he attributes to the whole man both of these opposing qualities which come from the opposing parts of him. For in this way there comes about a communication of attributes, for one and the same man is spiritual and carnal, righteous and a sinner, good and evil.

The good commanded by the Law, this he cannot do because of the resistance of the flesh. He does not want to lust, and he judges that it is a good thing not to lust, and yet he lusts and does not carry out his own will, and thus he is fighting with himself; but because the spirit and the flesh are so intimately bound together into one, although they completely disagree with each other, therefore he attributes to himself as a whole person the work of both of them, as if he were at the same time completely flesh and completely spirit.

Wretched man that I am! Who will deliver me from the body of this death? (v. 24). This even more clearly than the preceding statements shows that a spiritual man is speaking these words, for he laments and mourns and desires to be delivered. But surely no man except a spiritual man would say that he is wretched. For perfect knowledge of oneself is perfect humility, and perfect humility is perfect wisdom, and perfect wisdom is perfect spirituality. Therefore only the perfectly spiritual man says: "Wretched man that I am!"

But the carnal man does not desire to be liberated and set free but shudders terribly at the freedom which death brings, and he cannot recognize his own wretchedness. But when Paul says here, "Who will deliver me from the body of this death?" he is saying the same thing that he says elsewhere: "I desire to depart and be with Christ" (Philippians 1:23).

One and the same man at the same time serves the law of God and the law of sin, at the same time is righteous and sins! Therefore he also gives thanks that he serves the law of God, and he seeks mercy for having served the law of sin.

The saints at the same time as they are righteous are also sinners; righteous because they believe in Christ, whose righteousness covers them and is imputed to them, but sinners because they do not fulfill the Law, are not without concupiscence, and are like sick men under the care of a physician; they are sick in fact but healthy in hope and in the fact that they are beginning to be healthy, that is, they are "being healed."

He who does not earnestly strive to drive out sin certainly still possesses it, even if he has not committed any further sin for which he might be condemned. For we are not called to ease, but to a struggle against our passions. Therefore he who comes to confession should not think that he is laying down his burden so that he may lead a quiet life, but he should know that by putting down his burden he fights as a soldier of God and thus takes on another burden for God in opposition to the devil and to his own personal faults.

We are guilty and not guilty.

This twofold idea cannot be better explained than by the parable in the Gospel of the man who was left half dead (Luke 10:30ff.). For when the Samaritan had poured wine and oil on his wounds, he did not immediately recover, but he began to do so. Thus our sick man is both weak and getting well. Insofar as he is healthy, he desires to do good, but as a sick person he wants something else and is compelled to yield to his illness, which he himself does not actually want to do.

Let us force a rather crude example on unrealistic theologians: Suppose that a house which has fallen into disrepair is in the process of reconstruction, is then its construction and present condition one thing and its state of disrepair something else? It is one and the same thing. It can be said of the same house that because of its being under construction it is a house and that it is in the process of becoming a house, but because of its incompleteness it can at the same time be said that it is not yet a house and that it lacks what is proper to a house.

Thus "we who have the firstfruits of the Spirit" (Romans 8:23) "are become the beginning of God's creature," according to the apostle James (cf. 1:18), and "are built into a spiritual house" (1 Peter 2:5), and a structure thus "joined together grows into a holy temple in the Lord" (Ephesians 2:21).

The fruit, or result, of the Spirit's work in Christians is that we become more and more like Christ. Liars become honest. Adulterers become faithful. Gossips keep secrets in confidence. Cheaters play fair.

When Luther emphasizes the doctrine of the *simul*, he wants us to understand that in this life, saint and sinner always exist side by side. The sinful flesh inside still fights against the growth that can be seen on the outside. The old man and the new man continue to battle it out until the end.

The change in the fruit doesn't happen without struggle and pain, and the internal battle often leaves us wounded and scarred. Because of the battle, Christian growth often feels a lot more like failing than getting better. But the struggle is actually evidence of the growth. When it pains you that you talked behind your friend's back, that's evidence of the internal battle going on. When you experience guilt after hurting your spouse by saying exactly what you knew would get to him or her, that's evidence that the Spirit is going to war against the flesh inside of you.

Christian growth is not primarily about sinning less.

Christian growth is a war within us that is won by the Spirit through the Gospel. Because of the *simul*, you probably won't ever feel like you truly sin less. But as you grow, you'll realize more and more how big the problem of sin is. The moment you've put to death one habitual sin, you'll find sin that is much deeper than you realized. Because we never cease to be sinners even though God has made us saints, the more and more we grow, the more we understand exactly how "poor and wretched" we are.

Growth isn't about needing the cross less, it's about the cross doing its work daily. As we become acutely aware of what needs to be put to death, our daily lives transform. When we are reminded daily that the death and resurrection turns sinners into saints, we are changed. When we find ourselves exhausted by a fight we cannot win, we cry out, "Wretched man that I am! Who will deliver me from this body of death?" (Romans 7:24). The Gospel promises us that Jesus wins the fight we always lose. When daily battles leave us bloody and defeated, we can take heart, because Jesus has already won the war.

SUFFERING

Life is hard.

Regardless of a person's relationship with God, he'd be a liar if he suggested that life doesn't come with seasons of intense pain and difficulty. From the everyday struggles of life, such as a difficult job or rebellious kids, to life-altering moments, such as a diagnosis, a betrayal, or divorce papers, life is full of suffering.

It's this reality that makes Paul's words so difficult.

> We rejoice in our sufferings, knowing that suffering produces endurance, and endurance produces character, and character produces hope, and hope does not put us to shame, because God's love has been poured into our hearts through the Holy Spirit who has been given to us. (Romans 5:3–5)

Rejoice in suffering?

Seriously?

Are we really supposed to rejoice when somebody we love dies or when the doctor walks in with bad news? Who has ever rejoiced after a long-term relationship ends in a breakup? When was the last time our first response to being laid off was to rejoice?

I could manage an exhortation to "deal with suffering" or maybe more accurately "survive suffering." But "rejoice in suffering"!?

There is a kind of suffering that comes from His severity and another from His kindness. That suffering which comes from His kindness works, because of its nature, only things which are very good, as we see in the following, although by an accident something different may take place; but this is not His fault but the fault of him to whom it happens because of his weakness, for he does not know the true nature of his suffering and its power and working, but he judges and esteems it according to its outward appearance, that is, in a wrong way, since it ought to be adored as the very cross of Christ.

Of whatever quality suffering finds characteristics and people to be, such it makes them even more. Thus if a person is carnal, weak, blind, evil, irascible, arrogant, etc., when trial comes, he becomes more carnal, weaker, blinder, more evil, more irascible, more arrogant, etc.

Those people talk nonsense who attribute their bad temper or their impatience to that which causes them offense or suffering. For suffering does not make a person impatient but merely shows that he has been or is still impatient. Thus a person learns in suffering what kind of man he is.

> For I consider that the sufferings of this present time are not worth comparing with the glory that is to be revealed to us. For the creation waits with eager longing for the revealing of the sons of God. For the creation was subjected to futility, not willingly, but because of Him who subjected it, in hope that the creation itself will be set free from its bondage to corruption and obtain the freedom of the glory of the children of God. For we know that the whole creation has been groaning together in the pains of childbirth until now. And not only the creation, but we ourselves, who have the firstfruits of the Spirit, groan inwardly as we wait eagerly for adoption as sons, the redemption of our bodies. For in this hope we were saved. Now hope that is seen is not hope. For who hopes for what he sees? But if we hope for what we do not see, we wait for it with patience.

> Likewise the Spirit helps us in our weakness. For we do not know what to pray for as we ought, but the Spirit himself intercedes for us with groanings too deep for words. And He who searches hearts knows what is the mind of the Spirit, because the Spirit intercedes for the saints according to the will of God. (Romans 8:18–27)

It is not a bad sign, but a very good one, if things seem to turn out contrary to our requests. Just as it is not a good sign if everything turns out favorably for our requests.

The reason is that the excellence of God's counsel and will are far above our counsel and will, as Isaiah 55:8–9 says: "For My thoughts are not your thoughts, neither are your ways My ways, says the Lord. For as the heavens are higher than the earth, so are My ways higher than your ways and My thoughts than your thoughts." And Psalm 94:11: "The Lord knows the thoughts of men, that they are vain."

Hence it results that when we pray to God for something, whatever these things may be, and He hears our prayers and begins to give us what we wish, He gives in such a way that He contravenes all of our conceptions.

He does all this because it is the nature of God first to destroy and tear down whatever is in us before He gives us His good things, as the Scripture says: "The Lord makes poor and makes rich, He brings down to hell and raises up" (1 Samuel 2:7–6).

We are capable of receiving His works and His counsels only when our own counsels have ceased and our works have stopped and we are made purely passive before God.

In weakness, we learn how to depend. From birth, we struggle to learn independence, but suffering is the reminder that we can't make it on our own. Suffering is often the reality check that sometimes God allows us to face even more than we can handle—but never more than He can handle.

Therefore, when everything is hopeless for us and all things begin to go against our prayers and desires, then those unutterable groans begin. And then "the Spirit helps us in our weakness" (Romans 8:26). For unless the Spirit were helping, it would be impossible for us to bear this action of God by which He hears us and accomplishes what we pray for. Then the soul is told, "Be strong, wait for the Lord, and let your heart take courage and bear up under God" (Psalm 27:14). And again: "Be subject to the Lord and pray to Him," "and He will act" (Psalm 37:7, 5). What is said in Isaiah 28:21 takes place here: "He does a strange work in order to do His own work."

Therefore those who do not have this understanding of God and His will do as those do of whom it says in Psalm 106:13, 24:

We are capable of receiving His works and His counsels only when our own counsels have ceased and our works have stopped and we are made purely passive before God.

— MARTIN LUTHER

"They do not bear up under His counsel" and "they despised the pleasant land." These people trust in their own pious intention and presume that they are seeking, willing, and praying rightly and worthily for all things.

Therefore when what they have thought of does not immediately come to them, they go to pieces and fall into despair, thinking that God either does not hear them or does not wish to grant their requests, when they should have hoped all the more confidently, the more they saw everything go counter to their desires, for they know that they "are dust and that man is like grass" (Psalm 103:14–15). But they want to be like God, and they want their thoughts to be not beneath God but beside Him, absolutely conformed to His.

God always meets us when rock meets bottom. He promises to meet us in the place of despair. It doesn't matter whether we have been weakened by cancer, a hopeless search for love, or the betrayal of a friend, Jesus meets us in our suffering as the God who suffers with us.

Suffering isn't something to be sought after, yet in a profound way, suffering is something worth rejoicing over. When we're convinced that we don't have anything left, we have no choice but to depend on Jesus. When we give up our fight, we have no choice but to rely on Jesus to fight for us. When we realize we can't face something on our own, we have no choice but to finally trust that God can handle it.

Jesus doesn't wait for you to get through the suffering; He meets you in the midst of it. Jesus doesn't back away from the suffering; He enters into the blood and the bruises and promises to listen to you when you feel like you've lost it all.

Prayer in the midst of suffering is the desperate cry of the person who's given up. Prayer is the last grasp for somebody who knows she can't do it on her own. Prayer is offered when the one who suffers finds a confidence outside of himself and his situation and solely in the God who is with him.

Those who have the Spirit are helped by Him. Thus they do not lose hope but have confidence, even though they are aware of what goes contrary to what they have so sincerely prayed for.

He who seeks an advocate is confessing that he does not know how to speak or to pray as he ought, and he who needs a comforter confesses that he is certain that he is hopeless and cast down. This is how it is with us when God hears our prayers. For when we ask for nothing but things that are good and salutary and receive the contrary, we must necessarily be sad and afflicted. For all is lost and condemned. Therefore we need someone else to intervene for us, one who understands these things and prays for us and in the meantime sustains us so that we do not lose heart.

Suffering is hard. No matter what age we are or stage of life we are in, no matter what family situation we come from, and no matter how successful our career is, we will face suffering. Yet still, when we face suffering, we often find ourselves completely powerless, with no idea what to do.

Martin Luther suggested, "He who does not know Christ does not know God hidden in suffering."[13] Rabbi Shelomo ben Yitzhaki, a medieval French rabbi commonly called "Rashi," said, "When you look closely and for a long time, you discover things that are invisible to others."[14]

In the midst of the pain and hurt, God is hidden yet still at work. In the pain, when we are completely powerless, we have no other option but to rely on the One who has power over our situations. In the pain and hurt, even when we can't see anything good, there is One who is working for good.

And we know that for those who love God all things work together for good, for those who are called according to His purpose. For those whom He foreknew He also predestined to be conformed to the image of His Son, in order that He might be the firstborn among many brothers. And those whom He predestined He also called, and those whom He called He also justified, and those whom He justified He also glorified.

What then shall we say to these things? If God is for us, who can be against us? He who did not spare His own Son but gave Him up for us all, how will He not also with Him graciously give us all things? Who shall bring any charge against God's elect? It is God who justifies. Who is to condemn? Christ Jesus is the one who died—more than that, who was raised—who is at the right hand of God, who indeed is interceding for us. Who shall separate us from the love of Christ? Shall tribulation, or distress, or persecution, or famine, or nakedness, or danger, or sword? As it is written, "For Your sake we are being killed all the day long; we are regarded as sheep to be slaughtered."

13 AE 31:53.
14 Quoted by Lawrence Kushner in *God Was in This Place & I, i Did Not Know: Finding Self, Spirituality, and Ultimate Meaning* (Woodstock, VT: Jewish Lights Publishing, 1991), 22.

No, in all these things we are more than conquerors through Him who loved us. For I am sure that neither death nor life, nor angels nor rulers, nor things present nor things to come, nor powers, nor height nor depth, nor anything else in all creation, will be able to separate us from the love of God in Christ Jesus our Lord. (Romans 8:28–39)

We know that to those who love God, who according to His purpose, etc. On this text depends the entire passage which follows to the end of the chapter.

For there is no other reason or cause why numerous adversities and evils do not separate the saints from the love of God except the fact that they have not only been called but "called according to His purpose," and therefore to them alone and to no others "He works all things for good." For if it were not the purpose of God, and if our salvation depended upon our will and works, it would depend upon chance.

But now when he says: "Who will bring a charge? Who will condemn? Who will separate?" (vv. 33–35), he is showing that the elect are not saved by chance but by necessity. He shows that we are saved by His immutable love. And thereby He gives approval not to our will but to His own unchanging and firm will of predestination. For how could a man possibly break through all of these things in which he would lose hope a thousand times, unless the eternal and fixed love of God led him through them and the Spirit were present to aid our infirmity and to intercede for us with groanings which cannot be uttered?

Martin Luther likened these groanings to a soul struggle:

> [The feelings of fear] were so great and so much like hell that no tongue could adequately express them. . . . At such a time God seems terribly angry, and with Him the whole creation. At such a time, there is no flight, no comfort, within or without, but all things accuse. . . . All that remains is the starknaked desire for help and a terrible groaning, but [the soul] does not know where to turn for help. . . . Every corner of the soul is filled with the greatest bitterness, dread, trembling, and sorrow. (AE 31:129)

In the face of this great pain, God is hidden at work. When we are driven to our knees, the God who seems distant is actually present with us. When it seems like the world has turned against

MARTIN LUTHER

103

us, God is fighting for us. When it seems like the accuser wants to destroy us, Christ Himself stands in our place.

We may not see God in those moments, but He is there. And when the moment passes, we can look back and see it. God is there, even when it appears He is hidden.

CHAPTER 11

GRACE THAT CHANGES

When Luther comments on Romans, we find him primarily lecturing on topics such as justification by grace alone, the tension of a Christian being saint and sinner at the same time, and the distinction of Law and Gospel. Many of these subjects are what make Luther's writing so unique.

While Luther teaches on justification, he also understands something important that at times can be overlooked. Justification always effects our sanctification. In other words, the grace that saves us also changes us. And while the Law never gives us the power to do what it demands, the Gospel does. Christ who gives Himself freely for us is also at work in us producing a love for the people around us.

Making ethical decisions, caring for the poor and the hurting, and forgiving someone who hurt us are actions directly influenced by justification. In fact, the more we understand the depths of our justification, the more it changes us. Christians don't love more freely because they've been told they need to. Christians become more loving because they understand how much they've been

SANCTIFICATION

God's work of producing good works in the life of the Christian.

loved. Those who don't need to score points with God by their good works are freed to love and serve their neighbors because they are already completely and wholly loved by Jesus.

MARTIN LUTHER

The apostle is about to teach Christian ethics [in the verses below], and so no other concern is of such prime importance up to the end of the epistle as to eradicate our own wisdom and self-will. Therefore he begins immediately with this most noxious of all pests, because this alone under the subtle appearance of good works can again dissipate the spiritual birth and kill it by the very works themselves.

> I appeal to you therefore, brothers, by the mercies of God, to present your bodies as a living sacrifice, holy and acceptable to God, which is your spiritual worship. Do not be conformed to this world, but be transformed by the renewal of your mind, that by testing you may discern what is the will of God, what is good and acceptable and perfect. (Romans 12:1–2)

MARTIN LUTHER

He says here: "I appeal to you by the mercy of God," as if to say: "By the mercy which you have received, see to it that you do not receive it in vain, but rather 'present your bodies as a living sacrifice.' "

But be transformed. He is speaking of those people who already have begun to be Christians. Their life is not a static thing, but in movement from good to better, just as a sick man proceeds from sickness to health, as the Lord also indicates in the case of the half-dead man who was taken into the care of the Samaritan.

Just as there are five stages in the case of the things of nature: nonbeing, becoming, being, action, being acted upon . . . so also with the Spirit: nonbeing is a thing without a name and a man in his sins; becoming is justification; being is righteousness; action is doing and living righteously; being acted upon is to be made perfect and complete.

No one is so good that he does not become better, and no one so evil that he does not become worse, until at last we come to our final state. The apostle touches on this in a very effective way. He does not say: "Be transformed to the renewal," but *by the renewal,* or "through the renewal," or still better as it is in the Greek without a preposition: "Be transformed by the renewal of your mind."

He adds the expression "by the renewal" so that he should not appear to be teaching through the expression "transformation" something of the transformation of an unstable mind or some renewal of an outward worship, but rather renovation of the mind from day to day, more and more, in accord with the statement in 2 Corinthians 4:16: "Our inner nature is being renewed every day," and Ephesians 4:23: "Be renewed in the spirit of your minds."

A living sacrifice. The true sacrifice to God is not something outside us or belonging to us, nor something temporal or for the moment, but it is we ourselves, forever.

Some of the distinctions we've learned in previous chapters will become incredibly helpful now that we are back in the territory of the Law. The Law, which is good, is primarily focused on what we do. When we truly understand the weight of the Law in Romans, there is no sacrifice of our own effort that is "holy and pleasing" to God.

It's the sacrifice of Jesus that makes our works holy and pleasing to God. For example, loving our neighbors isn't holy and pleasing apart from faith. Only by grace through faith are we able to love our neighbors in fulfillment of what Romans demands. Our love for our neighbors is an act of worship produced by the work of Jesus.

MARTIN LUTHER

The word "holy" means something separated, or set apart, kept away from the profane, something which is removed from other uses and applied only to holy purposes worthy of God, something dedicated, as in Exodus 19:10: "Consecrate the people today and tomorrow, and let them wash their garments, etc." And again Joshua 3:5: "Sanctify yourselves; for tomorrow the Lord will do wonders among you." It is clear that the word "holy" means the same as clean or chaste, separated, particularly the cleanness which is owed to God.

It is nothing that we perform good works and live a pure life, if we thereby glorify ourselves; hence the expression follows *acceptable to God*. He says this in opposition to vainglory and pride which so often subvert our good deeds. For just as envy pursues someone else's happiness, so pride or vainglory pursue our own.

Whenever God gives us a new degree of grace, He gives in such a way that it conflicts with all our thinking and understanding. Thus he who then will not yield or change his thinking or wait, but repels God's grace and is impatient, never acquires this grace. Therefore the transformation of our mind is the most useful knowledge that believers in Christ can possess. And the preservation of one's own mind is the most harmful resistance to the Holy Spirit.

When Abraham was ordered to go out of his country and did not know the place where he was to go, this was surely contrary to his

Whenever God gives us a new degree of grace, He gives in such a way that it conflicts with all our thinking and understanding.

—MARTIN LUTHER

thinking. Likewise when he was commanded to sacrifice his son, this required a most noble transformation of the mind . . . ; and the will of God concerning Isaac looked sharp, displeasing, and hopeless; and yet afterwards it was proved to have been the best possible, full of blessing, perfect.

In the church God does nothing else but transform this mind.

Through God's words of Law and Gospel, the Spirit does a work of transformation on us. He speaks words of conviction that break us, and He speaks words of hope that renew and change us. While we at one point saw things one way, the transformation of God gives us new eyes to see the world around us in a new way.

Instead of "those people," we see neighbors who need to be loved.

Instead of an opportunity for revenge, we cherish the call to "love your enemies."

Instead of holding a grudge, we forgive seventy times seven times.

Instead of gossiping with our friends, we look for opportunities to speak words that always build up.

Luther continues to remind us that God is interested in changing our minds by showing how Paul contends on behalf of the Christians against a kind of servitude that is spiritual but very bad.

This is a matter of being subjected to the Law and all of its burdens, that is, to believe that it is necessary for salvation to fulfill all the external works of the Law. For they who think and believe this, remain slaves and will never be saved.

Transformation is the result of justification. Grace never saves us without also changing us. Good works will follow, but good works are not the source of our hope. Christians don't find assurance in a transformation inside of them, they find assurance outside of them—in the work of Christ on the cross. Christians don't find hope in how much they've changed; they find hope in Jesus' death and resurrection. Christians don't find peace in the quality of their good works; they find peace in knowing the work of Christ done for them.

A Christian's love for neighbor is not the result of Christian obligation. That's not love—it's obedience. A Christian's love for neighbor is the result of the love of Jesus overflowing and transforming the heart of the Christian into the heart of a servant.

They are the servants of the Law, and the Law rules over them because of this foolish faith and conscience of theirs. And such are all those who desire to be saved in some other way than through faith in Christ, for they are greatly concerned how they can satisfy the Law by their many works and their own righteousness. To be sure, the apostle and spiritual men also performed these works and still do so, but not because they have to but because they want to; not because the works are necessary but because they are permitted. But these hypocrites have tied themselves up in their good works as necessary works, and therefore they do them because they have to of necessity and not because they want to.

So how do we serve?

Because of the death and resurrection of Jesus, we don't need a spiritual scorecard of our works to make us look better before God. Our good works don't earn His favor. But this doesn't mean our good works aren't necessary.

Our neighbors need our good works. Jesus doesn't need our love and service, but our neighbors do. Jesus doesn't need our food in order to survive, but our neighbors might. Jesus doesn't need us to protect Him and care for Him, but our own children do need care and protection.

God gives us gifts and opportunities to serve the people around us—not because of His needs, but because of theirs.

> Owe no one anything, except to love each other, for the one who loves another has fulfilled the law. For the commandments, "You shall not commit adultery, You shall not murder, You shall not steal, You shall not covet," and any other commandment, are summed up in this word: "You shall love your neighbor as yourself." Love does no wrong to a neighbor; therefore love is the fulfilling of the law.

> Besides this you know the time, that the hour has come for you to wake from sleep. For salvation is nearer to us now than when we first believed. The night is far gone; the day is at hand. So then let us cast off the works of darkness and put on the armor of light. Let us walk properly as in the daytime, not in orgies and drunkenness, not in sexual immorality and sensuality, not in quarreling and jealousy. But put on the Lord Jesus Christ, and make no provision for the flesh, to gratify its desires. (Romans 13:8–14)

The commandment "You shall love your neighbor as yourself" is understood in a twofold manner, as it reads in Matthew 19:19 or as in Leviticus 19:18, where it reads: "Love your friend as yourself."

First, we can understand it in the sense that both the neighbor and one's own self are to be loved. But in another sense it can be understood that we are commanded to love only our neighbor, using our love for ourselves as the example. This is the better interpretation, because man with his natural sinfulness does love himself above all others, seeks his own in all matters, loves everything else for his own sake, even when he loves his neighbor or his friend, for he seeks his own in him.

Hence this is a most profound commandment, and each person must test himself according to it by means of a careful examination. For through this expression, "as yourself," every pretense of love is excluded.

Therefore this is the hardest commandment of all, if we really think about it. And thus it is that no one wishes to be robbed, harmed, killed, to be the victim of adultery, to be lied to, victimized by perjury, or have his property coveted. But if he does not feel the same way also about his neighbor, he is already guilty of breaking this command.

Therefore this commandment also includes the idea of Matthew 7:12: "So whatever you wish that men would do to you, do so to them; for this is the Law and the Prophets." Thus although this commandment when viewed in a superficial and general way seems quite a small matter, if we apply it to particular cases, it pours forth infinite salutary teachings and gives us faithful direction for all of our dealing. But the fact that this commandment is not observed and that we sin against it countless times and that it is ignored by those who are thoughtless proves that people do not apply it to their own actual undertakings but are content with their good intentions.

He who wishes to think seriously about this commandment and apply it ought not to depend on his own actions which are elicited from within, but rather he must compare all the acts, words, and thoughts of his whole life with this commandment as a rule and always say to himself about his neighbor: "What would you wish done to you by him?" And when he has seen this, let him also begin to do the same toward his neighbor, and immediately the contention, the detraction, the dissension will cease, and there will be present the whole host of virtues, every grace, every act of holiness, and as it says here, "the fulfilling of the Law."

For this is how Moses taught the children of Israel in Deuteronomy 6:6 ff.: "These words which I command you this day shall be upon your heart; and you shall teach them to your children, and you shall talk of them when you sit in your house, and when you walk by the way, and when you lie down, and when you rise." And then he continues by saying: "And you shall bind them as a sign upon your hand, and they shall be as frontlets between your eyes. And you shall write them on the doorposts of your house and on your gates." It was not the wish of Moses that we wear Pharisaic phylacteries, but saying that they are to be as "a sign upon your hand" means that all our efforts must be applied and directed to this end. And the expression "between your eyes" means that all our thoughts must be directed by these words, and the phrases "to write them on the doorposts of your house and on your gates" means that all our senses and particularly our tongue must be directed and applied according to these words.

He who would do this would come to a complete knowledge of his faults and to humility and fear of God; otherwise he remains secure and saintly in his own opinion. For he would often discover not only that he is sluggish in helping his neighbor—while at the same time he nevertheless finds that he wants everyone to be kindly affectioned, loving, and favorably disposed toward him—but that he himself is actually an enemy and a false brother toward his brothers, indeed, a detractor and full of every kind of sin.

There is no doubt that with these words also in this passage he is speaking of spiritual sleep, where the spirit is sleeping when it lives in sins and is content. Christ in many ways in the Gospel wakes us up against this kind of sleep, admonishing us that we must be watchful. And we must take note that he is not speaking of those people who are dead in the sin of unbelief, nor about those believers who are lying in mortal sin, but rather about Christians who are living lukewarm lives and are snoring in their smugness.

Of these people blessed Bernard says, "He who does not constantly hasten to repent says by this action that he does not need repentance."[15] And if he does not need repentance, he does not need mercy; and if he does not need mercy, then he does not need salvation. This is something which cannot happen, unless one is without sin, as God and His angels are.

Just as in the foregoing where he has instructed man with regard to himself, namely, that he be temperate, watchful, and chaste,

---

15 *Sermo II in vigil nativictatis Domini, Patrologia, Series Latina*, CLXXXIII, 90.

so here in this passage he is giving him instruction regarding his relationship with his neighbor, that they live together in peace, unity, and love.

The grace that saves you also changes you.

Peace, unity, and love are the products of grace changing a person. Forgiveness offered freely changes the peace in a person's relationships. Praying for your neighbor produces a different kind of unity in your relationship with him. Recognizing how much you've been loved produces a love that you couldn't manufacture.

No amount of effort or good intentions will change you from a selfish person to a self-sacrificial person. No amount of discipline will turn a me-centered heart into an others-centered heart. No sinful people by their own resolve will be able to love people the way that God calls them to love.

But the death and resurrection of Jesus will. It transforms the heart and the mind. It transforms conversations and relationships. The selfishness and the stubbornness inside of us are transformed into sacrifice and submission that can come only from outside of us.

GIFTS

∘ Remember when you were a child and you were told, "You can be whatever you want when you grow up"?

Did you discover that to be true?

I'm not suggesting that we start crushing the dreams of children, but I'm not really sure that there are limitless possibilities. When you are young, nothing is off limits, but reality as an adult is far different.

If you don't have the gifts or abilities to do certain things, you probably won't be able to do those things in your career.

If you don't have any gifts or abilities in engineering, you probably won't be an engineer.

If you don't have any musical ability, you probably won't become a musician.

If you can't dribble a basketball, you probably won't make the NBA.

If you have no patience for junior high students, you probably won't teach junior high math.

And if you can't balance a budget, you probably won't be a Chief Financial Officer.

You can't be anything you want to be. You can try anything you want to try and you can do a wide variety of activities, but you can't "be" just anything. You can be only what God has created you to be. If God doesn't call you to be a pastor, you won't be a pastor. If God doesn't call you to be a mother, you won't be a mother. If God doesn't gift you with the ability to teach, you probably won't be a teacher. If He doesn't endow you with leadership skills, you probably won't be a leader.

> For by the grace given to me I say to everyone among you not to think of himself more highly than he ought to think, but to think with sober judgment, each according to the measure of faith that God has assigned. For as in one body we have many members, and the members do not all have the same function, so we, though many, are one body in Christ, and individually members one of another. Having gifts that differ according to the grace given to us, let us use them: if prophecy, in proportion to our faith; if service, in our serving; the one who teaches, in his teaching; the one who exhorts, in his exhortation; the one who contributes, in generosity; the one who leads, with zeal; the one who does acts of mercy, with cheerfulness. (Romans 12:3–8)

MARTIN LUTHER

The term "measure of faith" can at first sight be understood as the measure or mode according to which faith is given in distinction to all other gifts. But here it cannot be understood in that sense, as is obvious from the fact that he states that different gifts are given according to this measure. Therefore we must understand the expression "measure of faith" in a second sense, that is, the measure of the gifts of faith, that is, in faith there are many gifts, and though believers live in the same faith, yet they have a different measure of the gifts of faith. And this is what he calls the measure of faith, because those who act outside of faith do not have these gifts and this measure. For although there is one faith, one Baptism, one church, one Lord, one Spirit, one God, nevertheless, there are various kinds of gifts.

At this point, and from here to the end of the epistle, he teaches how we should act toward our neighbor and explains at length this command to love our neighbor. But it is remarkable how such a clear and important teaching of such a great apostle, indeed of the Holy Spirit Himself, receives no attention.

We are busy with I don't know what kind of trifles in building churches, in increasing the wealth of the church, in piling up money, in multiplying ornamentation and gold and silver vessels, in installing organs, and in other forms of visible display. And the sum total of our piety consists of this; we are not at all concerned about the things the apostle here enjoins, to say nothing of the monstrous display of pride, ostentation, avarice, luxury, and ambition which are found in these activities.

Luther doesn't pull any punches here. God has gifted the Church in a variety of ways, yet she finds herself caught up in the things that don't matter. The Church gets so caught up in building individual churches that often she forgets to be the Church. The business of the Church—meetings, buildings, music, and numbers—often becomes the focus. The ministry of the Church—loving our neighbors—often gets pushed aside. Luther makes this point, not because he has a problem with church buildings or ornamental displays, but because he has a problem with churches that are bent in on themselves and therefore forget to look at the people they are trying to serve. God gives gifts to His Church not so they can build a great organization, but so they can "seek and save the lost" (Luke 19:10).

God has given you the gifts you need to be the person He created you to be. God doesn't need those gifts; it's not like He's waiting for those gifts to somehow change the way He sees you. But the people around you do need those gifts. Your neighbors need them. Your family needs them. Your church community needs them.

When Paul lists several gifts in this text, he's not creating an exhaustive list of all the possible gifts a Christian might have, but he is going to great lengths to make it clear that there are a variety of gifts that are all important to the Church. Luther does the same thing by examining these gifts. There are a variety of gifts; you might have some that are on the list and others that aren't on the list. The point is that God has gifted you to serve others with your gifts.

PROPHECY

He first turns his attention to the false prophets. For the gift of prophecy ought to be held and used "in proportion to our faith." And they act counter to this who prophesy on the basis of human judgment or according to the probable conjectures based on the workings and signs of nature, such as those who give counsel by the stars or from some plausible opinion of their own.

Thus a prophecy which is based only on experience or human argument is not true. . . . It is as if the apostle were saying: "If you wish to prophesy, do it in such a way that you do not go beyond faith, so that your prophesying can be in harmony with the peculiar quality of faith."

SERVICE

In Greek . . . "ministering." He who has the ministry has the grace of ministering. Let him carry out his duty in accordance with the proportion of faith and the measure of this grace.

The call either discovers grace or confers it. He who preaches without it "beats the air" (cf. 1 Corinthians 9:26) and glories in fruit existing only in his own foolish imagination. I will pass over those whom bishops and heads of orders everywhere nowadays are promoting to the pulpit, men who are utterly stupid and incompetent. Even if we should be willing to say that they are called and sent, we could not do so, because incompetent and unworthy men are being called, and this comes from the wrath of God, who because of our sins is taking His Word from us and is multiplying the number of empty talkers and garrulous chatterers.

TEACHING

He who teaches, he who has the grace of teaching, *in his teaching*, that is, let him do his work within the limits or proportion or measure of this grace.

Many people do have the ability to teach, even if they do not have great learning. Others have both, and they are the best teachers, such as St. Augustine, St. Ambrose, and St. Jerome. The man therefore who neglects this gift and involves himself in other matters sins against this command of the apostle, indeed, of God, especially those men who have been called and placed into such teaching positions.

EXHORTATION

He who exhorts, he who has the grace of exhorting, such as those who preach after faith has taken root, *in his exhortation*, let him not be presumptuous in other matters and neglect this.

The difference between teaching and exhortation is this, that teaching is directed to those who do not know, while exhortation applies to those who do know. The one builds the foundation, the other builds on it. He who teaches hands on knowledge; he who exhorts stimulates and moves his hearers in the direction of the fruit of the knowledge given to them.

GENEROSITY

He who contributes, who has the ability to contribute, [let him contribute] *in simplicity*, not in vainglory or with some other secret intent, because this goes beyond the grace of this service.

This man is attacked from two points.

In the first place, he is assailed when he gives in a relative sense and not absolutely, that is, with the idea that his gifts will bring him greater returns.

In the second place, such a man is attacked when superiors contribute to those beneath them or when equals give to equals. This gives much greater pleasure, obviously because of vainglory and boasting. For here "it is more blessed to give than to receive" (Acts 20:35). They are like God Himself, but only in their pride.

LEADERSHIP

He who rules, who directs others, [let him do so] *with carefulness*, with care for his service.

The primary measure of every master is his diligence, as the apostle here describes it. Moreover, a man cannot be diligent in the case of other people unless he is negligent of his own interests. For diligence produces negligence, perverse diligence makes evil negligence, but proper diligence a proper negligence. And thus he who rules must do so in diligence, that is, in negligence of his own interests.

MERCY

He who does acts of mercy, who has the ability to be merciful, [let him do so] *with cheerfulness*, not out of necessity or sadness.

This is different from what he has said above: "he who contributes, in simplicity." For in the former case it is a matter of giving to those from whom there is hope of being repaid, but here it refers to giving to the poor and needy.

He who is forced to come to the aid of the needy out of shame or some kind of threat does not show mercy with cheerfulness. Thus there are many people today who give substantial alms, but without any merit because they are unwilling and sad. Likewise there are those who give alms so that they may not be thought to be greedy or heartless or without mercy.

Paul writes, "[This] is your spiritual worship" (Romans 12:1). In using our gifts to serve our neighbor, we are worshiping the Giver of our gifts and the One who makes our service holy and pleasing. Our love for God is seen primarily in the love we have for one another.

Therefore let us not pass judgment on one another any longer, but rather decide never to put a stumbling block or hindrance in the way of a brother. I know and am persuaded in

the Lord Jesus that nothing is unclean in itself, but it is unclean for anyone who thinks it unclean. For if your brother is
grieved by what you eat, you are no longer walking in love. By
what you eat, do not destroy the one for whom Christ died. So
do not let what you regard as good be spoken of as evil. For
the kingdom of God is not a matter of eating and drinking but
of righteousness and peace and joy in the Holy Spirit. Whoever thus serves Christ is acceptable to God and approved
by men. So then let us pursue what makes for peace and for
mutual upbuilding.

Do not, for the sake of food, destroy the work of God. Everything is indeed clean, but it is wrong for anyone to make another stumble by what he eats. It is good not to eat meat or drink
wine or do anything that causes your brother to stumble. The
faith that you have, keep between yourself and God. Blessed
is the one who has no reason to pass judgment on himself for
what he approves. But whoever has doubts is condemned if
he eats, because the eating is not from faith. For whatever
does not proceed from faith is sin. (Romans 14:13–23)

This term "I am persuaded" is not to be understood in this passage
in the sense of "I hope," but in an absolute sense of "I am secure
and certain and very bold," or "daring," as he has also said above:
"Then Isaiah is so bold as to say" (Romans 10:20), that is, he speaks
with confidence and boldness.

It is as if he were saying: "Your presumption that the kingdom of
God is yours is in vain if you disturb the peace because of food and
are so eager to defend what you eat and drink, as if the kingdom of
God consisted in these things, as now is very frequently the case."
The outward food arouses more storms than the inward religion
produces peace, and they continue their disturbance during both
peace and war.

But [of] righteousness, as over against God, which comes through faith
or by believing; *and peace*, as over against our neighbor, which
comes about through love for one another and by receiving and
upholding one another; *and joy in the Holy Spirit*, as over against
oneself, which comes about through hope, by having trust in God
and not in those things which one does toward his neighbor or
toward God. Be pleasant toward yourself, peaceful toward your
neighbor, righteous before God.

Be pleasant toward yourself, peaceful toward your neighbor, righteous before God.

—MARTIN LUTHER

For whatever does not proceed from faith is sin. Here the apostle is speaking in a very general way regarding faith, and yet in so doing he is alluding to the singular faith which is directed toward Christ, outside of which there is no righteousness but only sin. Moreover, it is faith in God, faith in one's neighbor, faith in oneself.

By faith in God any person is made righteous, because he acknowledges that God is truthful, in whom he believes and puts his trust. And by faith in his neighbor he is called a faithful, true, and trustworthy man, having become over against his neighbor what God is to him. And this faith in the neighbor is also called an active faith, by which he believes in his neighbor. And the nature of this faith is that if a person acts differently from what he believes or if he has doubts about this neighbor, he offends against his neighbor, because he does not do for him what he has promised.

> We who are strong have an obligation to bear with the failings of the weak, and not to please ourselves. Let each of us please his neighbor for his good, to build him up. For Christ did not please Himself, but as it is written, "The reproaches of those who reproached You fell on Me." For whatever was written in former days was written for our instruction, that through endurance and through the encouragement of the Scriptures we might have hope. May the God of endurance and encouragement grant you to live in such harmony with one another, in accord with Christ Jesus, that together you may with one voice glorify the God and Father of our Lord Jesus Christ. Therefore welcome one another as Christ has welcomed you, for the glory of God. (Romans 15:1–7)

Love bears all men and "all things" (1 Corinthians 13:7).

This expression "to bear" means that one makes the sins of all his own and suffers with them. For this is what love does, and these are the words of love: "Who is weak, and I am not weak? Who is made to fall, and I am not indignant?" In the same way he encourages in Galatians 6:2: "Bear one another's burdens, and so fulfill the law of Christ."

Philippians 2:5–7: "Have this mind among yourselves, which you have in Christ Jesus, who, though He was in the form of God, did not count equality with God a thing to be grasped, but emptied Himself, taking the form of a servant."

It has been ordained: "Each must bear the shame of the other." And although it may be hard to bear the shame of another and to share in it when one is innocent, yet it is a good and meritorious act. And it will be easy, if one recognizes that Christ gladly bore our shame, even though it was hard for Him. Thus "none of us lives to himself" (Romans 14:7).

The most beautiful fools of all are those who forget that they themselves are the dirtiest of all when they inveigh against priests, monks, and women and impute to all of them what one person has done. These people do nothing but revile, judge, accuse, despise others. They have no mercy on others but rather rage against them, and nothing is clean but they themselves.

It is a characteristic of these people to be scornful over the unrighteousness of others rather than to rejoice over the fact that they are righteous; and they would not rejoice at all if others were as righteous as they are. For this would be very displeasing to them.

Christians are notorious for their judgment of others. The Barna Group, in a survey of adults who don't attend church, found that 72 percent believe the Church "is full of hypocrites."[16] From the media to personal relationships to the random meetings in our own church experiences, it's likely that most of us have encountered this stereotype.

Although this is a stereotype, it's one that is often true. Sin has made us all hypocritical. We tell our kids not to do something that we know we are guilty of doing. We talk about right and wrong during Bible study while knowing that we repeatedly choose the wrong thing when no one's looking. We talk with judgment and scorn about other people's sins, yet when it comes to our own sin, we have no problem justifying our behaviors.

This isn't a modern problem—Jesus repeatedly encountered the same problem with the Pharisees. It's this same problem that led Him to make bold accusations like, "Woe to you, scribes and Pharisees, hypocrites! For you are like whitewashed tombs, which outwardly appear beautiful, but within are full of dead people's bones and all uncleanness. So you also outwardly appear righteous to others, but within you are full of hypocrisy and lawlessness" (Matthew 23:27–28).

The Church has long said, "Love the sinner; hate the sin." But in the midst of hypocrisy, judgment, and lack of love, many have

---

16 Sarah Bruyn Jones, "72% Say Church Is Full of Hypocrites," *Tuscaloosa News*, January 19, 2008, www.religionnewsblog.com/20397/survey.

experienced just the opposite. As my friend Preston Sprinkle often says when speaking about this issue regarding homosexuality: "Love the sinner. Hate your own sin. We're in this together."[17]

When we are aware of both our own sin and the promise that Jesus gives Himself to sinners, we are set free to use our gifts and our opportunities to love our neighbors with no strings attached. God has given us gifts—mercy, leadership, generosity—not so that we might selfishly keep them to ourselves, but so that we might use them to love others.

MARTIN LUTHER

Charity is love not for oneself but for another.

As soon as the apostle rejected self-complacency, he immediately went on to teach that we should please our neighbor. Therefore to please our neighbor means not to please oneself.

Hence with all respect for the judgment of others and with reverence for the fathers, I want to say what is on my mind, even if I speak like a fool: This does not seem to be a correct understanding of the law of love toward our neighbor when it is interpreted in such a way that we say that in this commandment the person who loves is the model by which one loves his neighbor, obviously because the commandment says "as yourself."

Thus people conclude: It is necessary that you first love yourself and thus in keeping with this example of your love you then love your neighbor. And to support this they adduce the statement of the wise man (Ecclesiasticus 30:21), "Have pity on your soul, pleasing God," namely, by putting the emphasis on the pronoun "your," as if to say: "First pity your own soul and then your neighbor's."

I do not reject this interpretation, although I believe that the emphasis is on the word "soul," as if to say: "Do not spare your body, in order that the soul may be saved. Be cruel toward the Old Adam, in order that you may be merciful toward the new man." For "better is the wickedness of a man than a woman who does good" (Ecclesiasticus 42:14), that is, it is more salutary if the soul inflicts evil and injury on the flesh than if the flesh pets and flatters the soul or "does good," according to what seems "good" to it.

Therefore I believe that with this commandment "as yourself" man is not commanded to love himself but rather is shown the sinful love with which he does in fact love himself, as if to say: "You are completely curved in upon yourself and pointed toward love of

17 Preston writes about this idea in his book *People to Be Loved: Why Homosexuality Is Not Just an Issue* (Grand Rapids, MI: Zondervan), especially chapter 5.

yourself, a condition from which you will not be delivered unless you altogether cease loving yourself and, forgetting yourself, love your neighbor."

Our guilt has fallen upon Him, that is, He has paid the penalty for them and made satisfaction for us. If He had wanted to please Himself and love Himself, He surely would not have done what He did. But now He has loved us and hated and humiliated Himself, He has completely given Himself up for us. Thus love is the reason why our neighbor is not displeasing to us and why we can have patience with him. Love does not allow us to please ourselves, inasmuch as it is patient itself, and without it every haughtily righteous person is impatient and self-pleasing.

Jesus turns our inward curves out toward our neighbors. When selfishness has made us worship only what pleases us, Jesus is at work in us making us forget ourselves. Jesus gives us new sight as we see our neighbors the way He sees our neighbors.

He is glorified when sinners and the weak are received. For His glory lies in the fact that He is our benefactor. Therefore it is for His glory, that is, an occasion for His kindness, when those are brought to Him who will receive His blessing. Thus we are not to bring the strong, the holy, the wise. For in them God cannot be glorified, since He cannot be a blessing to them, for they do not need Him.

Instead of looking for what we can get from somebody, we begin to see people truly in need. Instead of seeing an opportunity for influence or good merits, we begin to see the hurting. When we are curved inward on ourselves, we try to get something from everyone we meet. But when we have everything we need in Christ, we are free to love our neighbors because we already have everything we need in Jesus.

Instead of seeing our gifts as tools to meet our own needs or secure our own worth, we can use our gifts for the good of those who really need them. Instead of falsely believing our gifts are necessary to gratify God, we can use our gifts freely knowing that God is already pleased. God gives us gifts so that we might love sacrificially, give generously, and forgive freely.

As Christians, we are free to love sinners like we have been loved because we don't need anything in return—we already have all we need in Christ.

CONCLUSION

We have no problem believing that we receive salvation through grace, but once we are saved we often believe the rest is up to us. We believe that the Christian life is about what we do more than what's been done. We believe that our salvation was won on the cross but that we can only keep hold of it through the daily grind of obedience.

In the first chapter of this book, we learned from Luther that grace is "a righteousness that comes completely from the outside." It's an alien work; we are completely passive recipients. And while we might give lip service to this theology, the daily reality of what Christians experience when they worship is "do more" and "try harder."

No wonder people are leaving the Church.

If the Christian life is about being better, people will inevitably leave the Church the moment they realize they'll always be failures. Christianity isn't about being better and failing less; Christianity is about God meeting you in the midst of your failures and giving everything for you.

When religion is about what you do for God and not about the God who meets you when you've hit the bottom, it's not preaching Jesus.

Unfortunately, you can find a lot of religion that sounds nothing like the Gospel.

So stupid is everybody today.

The question therefore is whether it is good to become a religious

If you think you cannot have salvation in any other way except by becoming a religious, do not even begin.

– MARTIN LUTHER

in our day. The answer is: If you think you cannot have salvation in any other way except by becoming a religious, do not even begin. For the proverb is so true: "Despair makes a monk," actually not a monk but a devil.

Therefore examine yourself when you pray, when you make a sacrifice, when you enter the choir or do anything else whether you would do the same thing if you had your liberty, and then discover who you are in the eyes of God.

When you are burdened by the weight of the Law and crushed by your inability to be better, Jesus in His death and resurrection lifts the burdens. Jesus gives what Luther called "a longed for remedy" when He forgives sins freely. Jesus offers peace when sin torments your conscience. Jesus fights for you when you've got no fight left. Jesus saves sinners, even the worst of them.

A WORD FOR PREACHERS

Not everyone should be a preacher.

James reminds us of this when he writes, "Not many of you should become teachers, my brothers, for you know that we who teach will be judged with greater strictness" (James 3:1).

Within our own spheres, we all will teach, preach, and spread the Gospel, but when it comes to being the one who teaches to and on behalf of the Church—this is not a job for everyone. Christians need pastors who will make known the Gospel week in and week out. We need pastors who are willing to be despised, rejected, and shamed for the sake of the message of Christ alone. We need pastors who are willing to speak of the gift of the Gospel despite what might come against them.

Paul in Romans 15:19–20 writes, "I have fulfilled the ministry of the gospel of Christ; and thus I make it my ambition to preach the gospel."

He plainly says in the Greek: "I have been ambitious to preach the Gospel."

We must note that to preach the Gospel was a despised and ignominious duty, just as it still is, void of all honor and glory, exposed to every kind of insult, reproach, persecution, etc., to such a degree that Christ says: "Whoever is ashamed of me before men, I will be ashamed of him before the angels of God" (cf. Luke 9:26).

Since preaching the Gospel is not a matter of honor, with marvelous and apostolic love he regards that which is its shame as

MARTIN LUTHER

being his glory, only in order that he may be of benefit to others. For to preach where Christ is known is not disgraceful, because there the first shame of the Gospel is endured and overcome. But where He is not yet known, the disgrace poured upon the Gospel is still new and very great.

He is also speaking in this context in [Romans] 1:14, when he says: "I am under obligation both to Greeks and to barbarians, both to the wise and to the foolish." And in 1:16: "For I am not ashamed of the Gospel," as if to say: "I consider preaching the Gospel as an office of honor, and I am ambitious for it, for the very reason that others abhor it because of its dishonor."

[Paul] strove with pious ambition to fulfill his office as if he alone wanted to bring the light to the Gentiles, a task in which he most strongly gave proof of his love. For the ambition to do good is truly rare and thoroughly apostolic. Moreover, to preach the Gospel is to bestow the greatest benefit, even if it is done through the greatest persecutions and enmities of the whole world. Therefore to strive as it were for this glory (and this is the strongest of all desires) of bringing the greatest benefit and blessing, and this as a free gift, and what a free gift it is, and to receive nothing but every kind of reproach for it—is this not something that is beyond man and truly apostolic, indeed a divine kind of ambition?

Think about this. The Gospel is an indescribable gift, which cannot be compared with any other riches, honors, or pleasures. Furthermore, he who gives good things, even to his enemies and those who render him evil in return, what is his benefit in comparison with the Gospel?

The Gospel is for all people. It doesn't pick and choose based on race or gender. It doesn't discriminate based on the severity of your sin. And it doesn't play favorites to the pious or the religious. Grace is the unmerited favor of God for all people; the only requirement is that you be a sinner.

> Therefore you have no excuse, O man, every one of you who judges. For in passing judgment on another you condemn yourself, because you, the judge, practice the very same things. We know that the judgment of God rightly falls on those who practice such things. Do you suppose, O man—you who judge those who practice such things and yet do them yourself—that you will escape the judgment of God? Or do you presume on the riches of His kindness and forbearance

and patience, not knowing that God's kindness is meant to lead you to repentance? But because of your hard and impenitent heart you are storing up wrath for yourself on the day of wrath when God's righteous judgment will be revealed.

He will render to each one according to his works: to those who by patience in well-doing seek for glory and honor and immortality, He will give eternal life; but for those who are self-seeking and do not obey the truth, but obey unrighteousness, there will be wrath and fury. There will be tribulation and distress for every human being who does evil, the Jew first and also the Greek, but glory and honor and peace for everyone who does good, the Jew first and also the Greek. For God shows no partiality. (Romans 2:1–11)

This text is interpreted in a threefold way.

First, it is applied to those who hold the public office of a judge and who on the basis of their office condemn and punish people whom they themselves resemble in evildoing.

These people the apostle calls and tries to awaken from their deep blindness. Just consider whether both our secular and spiritual leaders are not haughty, seekers of pleasure, adulterers, and, worse than that, thieves, disobedient to God and men, and originators of unjust wars, that is, mass murderers. And yet they continue to punish these crimes most severely in their subjects.

In the second place, this must also be understood as applying to those who secretly in their hearts are judging others. Yes, they also judge them with their mouth when they denounce them, and yet they are in every respect exactly like those whom they judge. We call it shameless when a conceited person criticizes another conceited person, when one glutton rebukes another, or one miser snaps at another. This shamelessness is so obvious that it looks stupid and ridiculous even to fools, yet there is a strange blindness about it, so that very many people suffer from this plague.

They are therefore convicted by their own words, "Judge not that you may not be judged" (Matthew 7:1), that is, so you do not bring the same judgment upon yourselves that you bring upon others.

In the third place, this passage speaks about those people who think that they are holy and, as I said, are affected by sin that is different from the one they are judging.

They act as if they were righteous because they do not do quite all the things other people are doing, and not rather as if they were unrighteous because they are doing some of the things which others are doing. They make so great a to-do about the good things they are doing that on account of them they cannot see their mistakes.

It is of those people that the apostle is particularly speaking here. To teach that type of people and to correct them is an extremely difficult task, for we should not call them shameless if they merely judge those faults of which in part at least they are free. And yet they do not understand or do not notice that they are unrighteous because they are doing what they are judging.

The apostle wants to call them back to understand themselves, and he begins to teach them that no one who is outside of Christ should be excepted from those sinners, no matter how good he may be and no matter how he sits in judgment over them, he always remains among them, even though he does not see it. He is always doing the same things that he is condemning, even if he does not believe that to be true.

Preachers, "Are you smoking what you're selling?"

I love how Robert Capon, Episcopal priest and author, describes this same thing:

> But preachers can't be that naughty or brave unless they're free from their own need for the dope of *acceptance*. And they won't be free of their need until they can trust the God who has already accepted them, in advance and dead as doornails, in Jesus. *Ergo*, the absolute indispensability of *trust in Jesus' Passion*: unless the faith of preachers is in that alone—and not in any other person, ecclesiastical institution, theological system, moral prescription, or master recipe for human loveliness—they will be of very little use in the pulpit.[18]

Preachers need more than just communication skills. Preachers need to know more than just how to explain a text or read the original languages. Preachers need more than just an artistic sense and an ability to tell stories.

It doesn't matter how gifted a preacher is if he hasn't been freed by the Gospel that he preaches. A preacher's faith is not in his own abilities or the church organization that he is creating—his faith is in the grace that he proclaims.

---

18 Robert Farrar Capon, *The Foolishness of Preaching: Proclaiming the Gospel against the Wisdom of the World* (Grand Rapids, MI: Eerdmans, 1997), 14.

MARTIN LUTHER

How is it possible that a person teaches another person and does not first know something himself or is not taught himself?

He who teaches must first know and be taught what he teaches others.

> But if you call yourself a Jew and rely on the law and boast in God and know His will and approve what is excellent, because you are instructed from the law; and if you are sure that you yourself are a guide to the blind, a light to those who are in darkness, an instructor of the foolish, a teacher of children, having in the law the embodiment of knowledge and truth—you then who teach others, do you not teach yourself? While you preach against stealing, do you steal? You who say that one must not commit adultery, do you commit adultery? You who abhor idols, do you rob temples? You who boast in the law dishonor God by breaking the law. For, as it is written, "The name of God is blasphemed among the Gentiles because of you."
>
> For circumcision indeed is of value if you obey the law, but if you break the law, your circumcision becomes uncircumcision. So, if a man who is uncircumcised keeps the precepts of the law, will not his uncircumcision be regarded as circumcision? Then he who is physically uncircumcised but keeps the law will condemn you who have the written code and circumcision but break the law. For no one is a Jew who is merely one outwardly, nor is circumcision outward and physical. But a Jew is one inwardly, and circumcision is a matter of the heart, by the Spirit, not by the letter. His praise is not from man but from God. (Romans 2:17–29)

MARTIN LUTHER

The apostle indicates very clearly that he is speaking here of the spiritual doctrine and instruction in the Law, in which those who are teaching others merely according to the letter are not instructing themselves . . . that the works of the Law must be done with a willing and pure heart.

Not only do pastors need to do the right things, but they also need to do the right things the right way and with the right motivations.

They cannot do the Law they teach unless they do it with a joyful and pure will . . . so that they do or do not keep the Law merely in the outward work but do or do not keep it also with their will and their heart, that is, that they are free of evil works, also of the sinful lust of the heart, not only in the perfection of work, and that they are ready for good works not only from bodily necessity but also willingness of mind.

So those people are teaching a correct and complete law, but they are not doing it and accomplishing it.

These burdens are the commandments of the Law, of which he has said above that they should keep them. But by their literal explanation they become burdens hard to bear, and then they kill and do not make alive.

The whole task of the apostle and of his Lord is to humiliate the proud and to bring them to a realization of this condition, to teach them that they need grace, to destroy their own righteousness so that in humility they will seek Christ and confess that they are sinners and thus receive grace and be saved.

The goal of the apostle here is the task of the preacher—to humiliate the proud so that they realize they need grace. The goal of the teacher is to expose the student to his sin so that he might be exposed to his Savior. The goal is that our hearers might realize that their sin is far worse than they ever imagined, yet grace is far greater than they ever thought possible.

The Law burdens and destroys, yet not for the sake of destruction itself. The teacher speaks the word of the Law so that grace might relieve the burdened sinner and bring healing to the destroyed, self-righteous sinner.

Jesus is for you. He is for your students. And His promises are given, no questions asked.

SCRIPTURE INDEX

SCRIPTURE INDEX